Best Ever Mission Stories

Best Ever Mission Stories

Charlotte Ishkanian

Pacific Press® Publishing Association
Nampa, Idaho
Oshawa, Ontario, Canada
www.pacificpress.com

Cover design by Michelle Petz
Cover art by Michelle Petz
Inside design by Steve Lanto

Additional copies of this book are available by calling
toll free 1-800-765-6955
or online at http://www.adventistbookcenter.com

Library of Congress Cataloging-in-Publication Data

Ishkanian, Charlotte, 1945-
Best ever mission stories : kids in action around the world /
Charlotte Ishkanian.
p. cm.
ISBN 13: 978-0-8163-2263-3
ISBN 10: 0-8163-2263-5
1. Seventh-day Adventists—Missions—Juvenile literature.
2. Missionaries—Biography—Juvenile literature. I. Title.
BV2495.I84 2008
266'.6732—dc22

2007052311

08 09 10 11 12 • 5 4 3 2 1

Dedication

To the children around the world who have shared their stories of loving Jesus. You've changed my life forever.

Contents

Contents

Northern Asia–Pacific Division

South American Division

South Pacific Division

Southern Africa–Indian Ocean Division

Southern Asia Division

Southern Asia–Pacific Division

Trans-European Division

West-Central Africa Division

East-Central Africa Division

A New Friend for Jesus

Kenya

Steve met a sad young man and made a friend for Jesus.

Steve is twelve years old. He lives in Kenya, a country in eastern Africa. One day as Steve and his family were walking along the river, they saw a man sitting in front of a little thatched hut. The man looked young, but his shoulders drooped like an old man's shoulders. They could tell he had been drinking.

A new friend

Steve learned that the man's name was Kibogo *(kee-BOH-goh)*. Steve and his parents visited Kibogo often when they walked along the river. Sometimes Kibogo was friendly; but when he had been drinking, his actions frightened Steve.

One day during family worship, Steve said, "We are supposed to help the poor. Kibogo has nothing but rags to wear. Can we give him some clothes?"

Mother and Father looked at each other. They did not have much money, but they had a home and clothes to wear. "Yes,"

Father said, "I think we can find something for Kibogo."

Clothes for Kibogo

Mother went to the marketplace and found a shirt, trousers, and sandals for Kibogo. That evening Father and Steve found Kibogo sitting outside his thatched hut. "We brought you something," Steve said, giving Kibogo the bag. "I hope they fit." Kibogo opened the bag and pulled out the shirt and trousers.

"Thank you," Kibogo said quietly. "Why did you do this?"

"Your old clothes are torn," Steve said. "I wanted you to have something new." Steve waited as Kibogo tried on his new shirt. It fit well. "You know, Kibogo," Steve said, "if you stop drinking and smoking, you could earn enough money to buy food and clothes yourself."

"I know," Kibogo said sadly. "I've tried to stop, but I can't."

Steve and his father encouraged Kibogo before they returned home. "How can we help him quit drinking?" Steve asked.

"I don't know," Father said. "We can encourage him and pray for him. But God and Kibogo have to do the rest."

Kibogo, the family project

Sometimes Steve took a plate of Mother's home-cooked food to Kibogo. Steve often found Kibogo listening to his portable radio outside his hut. One day when Steve and his father arrived, Kibogo was upset. He had heard a news report saying that several people who drank the locally brewed beer had died. "That's what I drink!" Kibogo said. "I don't want to die. What can I do? Can you help me stop drinking?"

Steve and his father visited Kibogo every day to encourage him and pray with him. "Only God can free you from these addictions," Father said. "Let God help you stop drinking."

A new family

Steve invited Kibogo to come to church, and one day he agreed to visit. When he arrived at the church, he was welcomed warmly. Steve and his parents sat with Kibogo to let him know that they were glad he was there. During testimony time, Kibogo stood and said, "I have been drinking for many years, but I want God to forgive me and take away the desire to drink." The church members hugged Kibogo and welcomed him to their family.

Kibogo started attending church every week. Steve was excited to see how God was changing Kibogo's life. One Sabbath at church, Kibogo stood and said, "I don't drink alcohol anymore. I want to follow Jesus and be baptized."

People in the church said, "Praise God! Hallelujah! Amen!" Steve was so happy he could not speak, so he smiled.

On the day that Kibogo was baptized, Steve was very excited. The pastor thanked Steve and his parents for being Kibogo's friends and helping him find Jesus.

Kibogo, God's friend

Kibogo still lives in his small hut. But now he works at a regular job and is saving his money for a new house.

"Kibogo is my friend," Steve says. "God is our Father, so we are brothers. Sometimes we go fishing together on Sundays."

Today Kibogo is a church elder. He tells others about Jesus, just as Steve told him about Jesus.

You can tell others about Jesus too. Tell people who live near you that God can change their lives, just as He changed Kibogo's life.

Mwema's Mission

Democratic Republic of the Congo

A boy's dream to share God's love with others came true sooner than he thought.

Mwema *(mm-WEE-mah)* lives in the eastern part of the Democratic Republic of the Congo, near the border with Rwanda. One day he sat near his mother as she was cooking the family's dinner of rice with vegetables. "I want to be a pastor and lead many people to Jesus," he said.

Mwema's mother stopped stirring the big pot of steaming vegetables and smiled at her son. "How did you decide that?"

"Last year when we had the meetings at church, I listened to the speaker talk about Jesus. He told us that everyone who loves Jesus should tell other people about God's love. I want to do that. I want to start now, but I don't know what to do."

"Why don't you talk to the pastor?" Mother suggested. "He should have some good ideas."

The children's Bible club

Mwema told the pastor about his dream. The pastor asked him what he was doing to share God's love with others. "I have started a children's Bible club in my yard," Mwema said. "We—my brothers and sisters and some friends and I—meet three times a week, on Friday night, Sabbath afternoon, and Sunday evening, to tell Bible stories, sing songs, and pray with other children. Sometimes we play Bible games. Last week we had twenty-six children between nine and thirteen years old. My father gave us some Bible pictures to use, and he helps me prepare my stories to tell. Now, some of the older children lead the songs or tell a story," Mwema said.

The pastor leaned back in his chair. "You have made a great start," the pastor said, smiling. "It sounds as if you have done a fine job making friends who might like to attend evangelistic meetings. If you would like to hold meetings, I will help you."

Mwema thanked the pastor and hurried to tell his family. "The pastor said we should hold evangelistic meetings, just like the ones we had in our church last year!" Mwema said. "I want to do that."

Evangelistic meetings

It was vacation time, and Mwema had lots of time to devote to his Bible-club activities. The group continued to grow as children invited their friends. Mwema asked his father to help him prepare his sermons for the planned evangelistic meetings. He urged the children to invite their friends and their parents to the meetings. And every spare minute, Mwema worked to memorize the sermons his father had helped him write.

The time finally came for the evangelistic meetings, and Mwema was ready. Every afternoon for three weeks, children and their parents came to the clearing to listen to Mwema preach about God's great love for them and about His gift of Jesus. Mwema invited the children and the adults to give their lives to Jesus, and many did. A large number of the young people asked to be baptized, but many of the children were too young to be baptized or could not get their parents' permission. Even Mwema was too young to be baptized.

Mwema was disappointed that only four of the people who had come to the meetings and had decided to follow Jesus could be baptized. But the pastor encouraged him. "You've sown some good seeds, Mwema. We must continue to water those seeds, and one day we will see a good harvest." Mwema hoped that when he was old enough to be baptized, some of his Bible-club members would join him.

Mwema's dream

Soon after the evangelistic meetings ended, Mwema and his older brother packed their bags and boarded a bus. They were going to study at the Adventist school that is a day's bus ride from their home. Mwema was not afraid to leave home, but he was sorry he had to leave his friends and the children's Bible club. Many of the children who had attended the Bible club were leaving home to attend other schools too, and there would be no leader during the school year.

"When I return home from school, I want to start the children's Bible club again," Mwema says. "I have not given up my dream to share God's love with others."

Do you think Mwema will be a good pastor one day? He says it is easy to be an evangelist. All you have to do is share God's love with your friends, your playmates, and your family. It's that easy!

Euro-Africa Division

Making Friends for Jesus

France

Two young boys shared God's love with other people, and now those people are worshiping God.

Let's meet two boys who live in France. The boys, Kylian *(KEE-lee-ahn)* and Virgil *(VIHR-jehl)*, are in the same class at the Adventist school in Collonges *(koh-LOHNJ)*, France, a town on the border of Switzerland.

A boy, a book, and a blessing

One day not long ago, two young women came to visit Kylian's mother. They sat outside, talking and enjoying the warm day. Kylian noticed that the two young women were smoking. He watched them for a few minutes; then he told them, "You should not smoke; it can give you cancer." The young women were surprised at Kylian's comment, but they did not look angry.

Kylian remembered he had a book that tells about taking care of our bodies. He ran to his room, found the book, and showed it to his mother's friends. The two young women looked at the book while Kylian rode away on his bicycle.

The next day his mother's friends came to visit again. Kylian invited them to come to church with his family. He did not know what they would say, but they smiled and agreed to go. Now it was Kylian's turn to smile!

Mother's friends liked the worship service and asked to attend again. The young women have come to church almost every Sabbath since then. They want to join God's family.

Kylian and his mother are happy that Mother's young friends are following Jesus. Kylian says, "I know that I don't have to be afraid to tell others that God loves them. I can invite others to church, and so can you!"

Virgil's special friend

Virgil is Kylian's friend. He, too, has shared God's love with someone, his special friend Jean Luc *(John Luke)*. Virgil met Jean Luc when they were playing in a park one day. The boys liked playing together and became good friends. They often asked their parents to take them to the park together or to one another's house. In time, the boys' parents became friends too.

Then Virgil's family moved away to another town, an hour's drive from Jean Luc. Virgil missed his best friend and asked his parents to take him to see Jean Luc. One Friday after school, Jean Luc came to spend the weekend with Virgil. On Sabbath morning the family put on their best clothes and went to church. Jean Luc had never been to church with Virgil, but he liked Sabbath School a lot, especially the stories about Bible heroes.

When it was time for Jean Luc to go home, he asked Virgil's parents to let him come again and stay overnight so he could go to church with them another time. Virgil's parents agreed. Later that day Jean Luc told his parents about Virgil's church. Although Jean Luc's family did not go to church, they were willing to let Jean Luc go to church with Virgil.

Before long, Jean Luc visited Virgil's home again. The boys went to Sabbath School and church together, and later they enjoyed a nice afternoon walk. When Jean Luc returned home, he asked his parents to take him to church on Sabbath. His parents decided to visit the Adventist church in their town to see why their son liked it so much. Now the whole family goes to church every Sabbath.

Virgil is happy to know that his friend is going to church with his own family.

"I am glad that I invited Jean Luc to go to church with us," Virgil says. "Now he is learning about Jesus. That makes one more person—no, three more persons—who are learning about God. My parents say that I am a missionary because I invited my friend to church. Now I am looking for someone else to invite."

We can be missionaries, just like Kylian and Virgil. We can invite our friends, our neighbors, and even our family members to come to church with us. Who knows what will happen? Maybe our church will soon be full of people who say, "A child invited me to come."

Samuel's Special Project

We can serve God in many ways—with our voices, with our hands, and with our money.

Samuel lives in Germany. He has gone to church all his life, and he knows that it is important to give offerings to help others learn about Jesus.

Samuel's parents give him an allowance, and ever since he was a small boy Samuel has been careful to count out 10 percent for God. Then he counts out more to give as an offering. The rest of his allowance he can spend as he wishes.

His allowance is not a lot of money, but it allows him to buy school supplies and a few other things. Because Samuel likes to swim and snorkel, he spent some of his allowance on a face mask, swim fins, and a breathing tube, called a snorkel. He enjoys going snorkeling in the summer, so he saves his money all winter so he will have enough to pay for new equipment or fees when summer comes.

The *Voice of Hope* teacher

One day a visitor spoke in Samuel's church. The visitor was Thomas, a man from the *Voice of Hope* radio program in Germany. Samuel listened carefully as Thomas talked about people who study the Bible through the *Voice of Hope*'s Bible lessons that are sent through the mail. When Samuel learned that even children can take a Bible course, he leaned forward to listen.

Thomas explained that the work of the *Voice of Hope* depends on donations from believers who want others to know that Jesus loves them. Samuel was sure that Thomas looked straight at him when he said, "Even children help support the *Voice of Hope*." Then Thomas invited the children in church to sign up to take a *Voice of Hope* Bible course.

Samuel and many other children stayed after church to sign up for the Bible lessons that Thomas offered. Samuel filled out the enrollment card, and his mother mailed it. A few weeks later, Samuel's first Bible lesson came in the mail. Samuel sat down and read the lesson and answered the questions. Then he placed the lesson in the envelope. But before he sealed it, he wrote a letter to Thomas.

Samuel's promise

In the letter Samuel said, "Thank you for coming to our church and telling us about the Bible lessons. You said that you need donations for your work. I want more people to know about Jesus, so I am sending some money. Please use it to help others learn about Jesus. I want to send you some money every time I write. Your friend, Samuel." Then Samuel tucked ten euros (about US$12.30) into the envelope. This was his entire month's allowance after he returned tithe.

When Thomas received the letter and the donation, he was very happy. He knew that for a child, ten euros is a lot of money. Thomas wrote Samuel a nice letter, thanking him for his donation and telling him that the money would help many children learn about Jesus.

Every month after that, Samuel sent a donation to the *Voice of Hope*. Sometimes it was ten euros, and sometimes it was less. When he sent less, Samuel explained that he needed to buy school supplies or some other important item. And every time Samuel wrote, Thomas thanked him and told him that God would bless him.

Prayer request

One month Samuel wrote a different letter to send with his lesson. He told Thomas that he had broken his foot and that it was not healing right. He told Thomas that his foot hurt a lot, and he asked Thomas to pray for him. Thomas wrote back and said that the entire staff of *Voice of Hope* was praying that Samuel's foot would heal quickly.

Samuel continues to send money to the *Voice of Hope* each month. And he continues to study the *Voice of Hope*'s Bible lessons. Now his younger brother also is studying the Bible with the *Voice of Hope*.

"I am a Jesus fan!" Samuel says. "And I want other children to be Jesus fans too."

We all can be Jesus fans and tell others that God loves them. We can tell people whom we meet in the store, at school, or on the bus about Jesus. And we can give our offering to mission every week in church. That way, people we don't know will have a chance to learn that Jesus loves them.

Euro-Asia Division

A Real Family

Moldova

*Marina loved Granny Zina and Grandpa Vania so much. She would do
anything to help them to learn to love Jesus too.*

Marina and her mother lived in a little village in the country of Moldova *(mohl-DOH-vah)* in Europe. Marina's mother worked on a farm, but life was difficult; and no matter how hard Mother worked, she could not earn enough money to buy the things they needed. Finally Mother and Marina moved to a small town where Mother could find a better job.

Starting over

Mother found work, and she and Marina rented a room in the home of an older couple whom they called Grandpa Vania *(VAHN-yah)* and Granny Zina *(ZEE-nah)*. Mother was delighted when she found a little church close enough to their new home that she and Marina could walk to worship on Sabbaths.

Marina loved Grandpa Vania and Granny Zina. She loved to spend time with them, but when Mother invited them to church, they refused to go. "We have our own religion," they told Mother. "We are not interested in your church."

Marina often asked Granny Zina to tell her a story, and Granny gladly did. But one day when Marina asked for a story, Granny sighed, "I can't think of any more stories, child." With that, Marina ran to get her children's Bible. She gave it to Granny Zina. "Read me a story from the Bible, Granny," Marina said. Marina's Bible had pictures in it, and Granny found a picture and began reading her the story. Sometimes when Granny told the stories instead of reading them, Marina noticed that Granny told part of it wrong. Then Marina would say, "That is not in the story, Granny."

That Book in the trunk

Granny realized that she did not know the Bible as well as Marina did. So, one day she went to a trunk in the attic where she kept her old clothes. She dug through it and found her old Bible and dusted it off. She had not read it in years, but now she wanted to read it, so she would have more stories to tell Marina. She began reading a little of it every day.

As Granny read her Bible, she began discovering things she had never known before, such as God's commandment to remember the Sabbath day. She wondered what else was in the Bible that she had not heard about in church. Granny's heart began to soften as she read about God's love. She began joining Marina and her mother when they knelt to pray.

Grandpa's garden

One day Marina found Grandpa Vania weeding in the garden. She watched him a while; then she said, "In heaven there will be beautiful gardens, and they won't have bugs or caterpillars or weeds in them. I want you to be in heaven with Mommy and me, Grandpa. I will pray that you want to go to heaven, but you have to pray too, so Jesus will know that you want to go to heaven."

With that Marina ran to her room to pray, leaving Grandpa Vania to think about what she had said. *What if what Marina said is true?* Grandpa Vania thought. *What if I won't go to heaven?* After that, Grandpa listened more carefully when Marina talked about God. Then one day when Marina and Mother and Granny Zina prepared to pray, Grandpa joined them. Grandpa was not sure how to pray, so Marina helped him.

The invitation

New Year's Day was approaching, and Marina's church planned a special celebration. Marina invited Granny and Grandpa to go. At first they hesitated, but Marina begged, "Please, come. They will tell about Jesus during the program, and if you do not come, you will miss the chance to learn about Him." Granny and Grandpa agreed to go, and Marina was so excited! At the program, Marina sat between Granny and Grandpa.

On the way home, Marina told Granny and Grandpa, "Now you can come with us on Sabbath too!" Mother had warned Marina that Granny and Grandpa might not want to attend church on Sabbath. But Marina was sure they would if she invited them.

A Real Family

On Sabbath morning Marina ran to Granny Zina and Grandpa Vania and said, "Get ready, please, or we will be late for church." Granny did not want to disappoint Marina, so she and Grandpa quickly dressed and walked to church with them.

Granny and Grandpa continued to attend church with Marina and her mother, and before too many months, they asked Jesus to come into their hearts. Now Marina knows that Grandpa Vania and Granny Zina will be in heaven with them. And what could be better than the whole family spending eternity together?

The Girl Who Did Not Laugh

Ukraine

When the other children laughed at Vladimir, why didn't Julia laugh?

Vladimir *(vlah-DEE-meer)* and his family live in a little town in Ukraine, a country in south eastern Europe. His father is a shoemaker, and his mother is a teacher. The family has a big garden full of vegetables and fruit. They also have chickens, geese, ducks, and goats. Vladimir helps his parents weed the garden and care for the animals. There is little time to play, but Vladimir does not mind. He likes to help his parents.

Vladimir and his family pray and read the Bible together. They love to tell others about Jesus' love. Vladimir likes to play the guitar and sing; he especially likes songs about God. Vladimir wants Jesus to come again soon. But he knows that Jesus will not come until everyone has had a chance to hear about Jesus and choose whether they want to live with Him forever. Whenever he can, Vladimir shares his love for Jesus with people he meets— with his classmates and with people he meets on the train, while waiting for the bus, or while walking along the street.

The assignment

One day his teacher told the students to read something they liked and prepare to tell the class about what they had read. Vladimir decided to read the Sermon on the Mount from the Bible. He read it several times to be sure he remembered all of it.

The next day the children stood and reported to the class about what they had read. When it was Vladimir's turn, he stood and told about Jesus' famous sermon. The classroom was silent as he began explaining what Jesus taught long ago. Then suddenly someone started to laugh. Then other children laughed. Vladimir continued his report. The teacher told the students to be quiet, but some children continued to snicker at Vladimir. Vladimir felt sad that his friends did not respect Jesus. He did not understand why they laughed at God's words.

Julia's interest

But one girl in class did not laugh; she sat quietly and listened. After class Julia *(YOOL-yah)* told Vladimir that she liked his report. Then she asked if he had a book about Jesus that she could read. Vladimir reached into his backpack and pulled out his New Testament and gave it to Julia.

That evening Vladimir told his parents what had happened in class. He told them how the children had laughed but how Julia wanted to know more about Jesus. "We must pray for the children who laughed," Mother suggested. "And we will pray for Julia too."

That same evening Julia told her mother what had happened at school. She showed her mother the New Testament that Vladimir had given her. Mother and Julia read the New

Testament together. They both wanted to know about God.

A few days later Vladimir gave Julia another book, then another. Julia and her mother read the books together. They were glad to learn more about Jesus.

New friends, new faith

Vladimir invited Julia and her mother to meet his parents. The two families became friends. They went on hikes, had picnics, and spent quiet times just talking. Julia liked to sing while Vladimir played his guitar.

Julia and her mother asked a lot of questions about God, and Vladimir's family happily answered each question. "What is the difference between our traditional Christian faith and the Seventh-day Adventist faith?" Julia's mother asked. Vladimir's parents explained that Seventh-day Adventists try to follow the Bible in everything they believe and do. They showed her from the Bible why they worship on Saturday and why they live as they do.

Julia and her mother began attending worship with Vladimir's family. A few months later they gave their lives to Jesus and were baptized. Now Julia and her mother worship God and thank Him for everything. They are happy that Vladimir did not stop talking that day in class when the other children laughed at him.

Vladimir is glad that he helped two people to be part of God's family. He likes being a missionary and sharing God's love with people who do not know about Jesus. He still tells people he meets about God's love, whether it's at school, on the street, or in his home. If we all follow Vladimir's example, soon everyone will have heard that God loves them, and we can go to heaven. Wouldn't that be wonderful?

Inter-American
Division

Carlos's Plan

Venezuela

Carlos wished his father loved Jesus as he did. Then Carlos found a way to help him.

Carlos lives in Venezuela, a country on the northern coast of South America. He is ten years old and in the sixth grade. Carlos loves to play baseball and soccer and eat apple pie and *fororo (foh-ROH-roh),* a porridge made from corn and sweetened with brown sugar.

Praying for Daddy

Carlos has loved Bible stories for as long as he can remember. When he was small, his grandmother gave him a set of Bible story books. Every day, Carlos would ask his father to read him a story from the Bible story books. He heard the stories so many times that he almost had them memorized. Sometimes when his mother would try to shorten the stories by telling them in her own words, Carlos wasn't fooled. He would say, "No, Mommy, you left out part of it. Tell the whole story, just like it is in the Bible book."

Carlos and Mother went to church every week. But Carlos's dad did not go with them. He worked out of town a lot, and when he came home, he said that he was too busy or too tired to go to church. But Carlos never stopped asking his dad to go to church with Mother and him. "Please, Daddy," Carlos would say, "come to church with us. I want you there so much!" But Daddy kept making excuses. He always had other things to do.

Carlos felt sad that his father would not go to church with them, but he prayed for him every day. "Dear Jesus, please help Daddy to love You," he prayed. "Help him to want to come to church with us."

Carlos becomes a preacher

When Carlos was nine years old, he heard about the child-preacher clubs, where children meet and learn how to present a sermon or a short talk. They practice talking clearly and loudly enough so everyone can hear them. Carlos joined the child-preacher club in his church so he could learn how to preach. The pastor's wife helped the children learn their sermons. She showed them how to stand and what to do with their hands as they talked. And the children practiced giving a sermon until they could do it perfectly.

One day Carlos told his dad, "I want to be a child preacher. I've joined a club to learn how to do it, but I need someone to coach me at home. Will you help me, Daddy?"

"I don't know how I could help," Daddy said.

"I'll tell you what I want to say, and you write it down for me so that it sounds right," Carlos suggested. "Then when I learn my sermon, you can help me practice."

Daddy helps Carlos

"OK," Daddy said. "I'll help you all I can." The church planned to have youth Bible meetings, and Carlos was chosen to present two of the sermons. Carlos and Daddy worked together on Carlos's sermons, and soon Carlos could present his sermons without looking at his notes.

Soon the day came for the evangelistic meetings to begin. Daddy was home for once, and Carlos eagerly told him, "Daddy, please come to the meetings to hear me preach! And if you come every night, you can hear my friends preach too."

"OK," Daddy promised. "I'll be there." After all, what father wouldn't want to hear his son preach?

When it was time for Carlos to speak, he stood tall and spoke loudly and clearly. Daddy was so proud of Carlos!

The next night Carlos dressed for the program. But he found his dad was not ready to go. "Aren't you going to the meeting?" he asked. Daddy said he did not want to go that evening but that he would go the next time Carlos spoke. "But, Daddy," Carlos pleaded, "please come to all the meetings and support all the children who are speaking. I will have part in tonight's meeting, even though I am not preaching the sermon."

Daddy smiled and went to change clothes. He did not miss a single one of the meetings. On the last evening of the meetings, the speaker invited those who wanted to follow Jesus to stand up. Carlos stood up, and his dad stood up too.

Mother smiled through tears when she saw Carlos and his father standing together.

Several months later Carlos and his dad were baptized together. How happy Carlos is that now the whole family worships God together.

Carlos has a message for boys and girls everywhere. "If you want to see changes in your life, ask God to help you. And if your parents are not Christians, invite them to come to church with you. Pray for them and ask them to read the Bible with you and pray with you. Let your parents see that you love Jesus with all your heart, and tell them how important it is for them to do the same. That's what I did, and it worked. I think it will work for you too."

Kenia's Bible Club

Honduras

Kenia wanted her friends to learn about Jesus, so she led her own Bible Club.

Kenia *(KEN-yah)* is ten years old. She lives in northern Honduras. She likes school and enjoys riding her bicycle. She is a typical ten-year-old girl, don't you think? But Kenia does something most other ten-year-olds don't do: she leads her own Bible club every week.

Gift Bible

Kenia spends her weekends with her aunt and uncle. When she was nine years old, she learned that the Adventist church near her uncle's home was holding special Bible classes and that anyone who went every night would receive a gift Bible. Kenia wanted to go, but she could go only on the weekends. So Kenia asked her aunt, "Please go to the meetings every night so I can get the Bible." Her aunt agreed to go during the week, and Kenia went with her on the weekends. In two weeks Kenia had her own Bible.

Kenia listened carefully to the speaker and studied the Bible lessons that were given out each evening. Kenia began attending the Adventist church on Sabbath mornings too.

Kenia's parents were glad that Kenia was attending church. She invited her parents to come with her, but her father had to work and could not go. She asked them if she could be baptized, and they gave their permission.

Vacation Bible School

When Kenia learned that the church was planning to hold a Vacation Bible School, she stayed with her aunt during the week so she could attend the programs. She loved the crafts and the songs, but she especially loved the Bible stories. When Vacation Bible School ended, Kenia was sad it was over. Then she had an idea. She asked Mrs. Eppy, the woman who had led the Vacation Bible School program, an unusual question. "Mrs. Eppy," she said, "may I borrow the Vacation Bible School materials? I want to hold a Vacation Bible School for my friends."

Mrs. Eppy was surprised because Kenia was so young. She wondered how Kenia could plan an entire Vacation Bible School program without any help. But Kenia was determined, and finally Mrs. Eppy agreed to bring the materials to her house and help her plan the program.

Kenia invited the neighborhood children to her Vacation Bible School. She practiced the songs, learned the stories, and prepared the pictures that went with the stories. Mrs. Eppy helped her a little, but Kenia did most of the work herself.

Seventeen children came to Kenia's Vacation Bible School. Kenia taught them the songs she had learned and told them the stories that she had prepared. Vacation Bible School lasted a week, and the children loved it. When it was over, everyone felt a little sad.

Friends of Jesus club

On Sabbath Kenia found Mrs. Eppy and asked another question. "Please, can you help me start a Friends of Jesus Bible club for the children who came to Vacation Bible School?"

Mrs. Eppy smiled. She knew that Kenia could do it, so she gave her the materials she would need to start her own Friends of Jesus club.

Every Monday afternoon, Mrs. Eppy went to Kenia's house to help her hold the Friends of Jesus club meeting. Then on Tuesday Kenia had another club meeting without Mrs. Eppy's help. As many as ten children come to Kenia's club meetings. Kenia teaches them, using only a book of stories and a picture roll, but the children love it. Nearly all of the children who come are Kenia's age, and some are even older—ten to fourteen years. And one of Kenia's students has been baptized because of her Bible club.

When the church learned what Kenia was doing in her neighborhood, they asked her and her aunt to teach the children's Sabbath School class in the church. Kenia leads the singing and the prayer, and her aunt tells the Bible story. Why does she do all of this? "Because I love Jesus, and He loves me," Kenia says.

Kenia hopes that soon there will be an Adventist church in her own neighborhood, and if necessary, she plans to organize it herself. Don't be surprised if she does. She has made a good start with her Friends of Jesus Bible club.

North American Division

David's Birthday Party Project

United States

David wanted to be a missionary in Alaska, and one day he found a way.

"Have you decided which state to choose for your report?" David's mother asked as she came into his room. Nine-year-old David studied the map of North America.

"Alaska," he said. "I want to study Alaska. It's a neat state. Maybe someday I can go there as a missionary." David traced the state's outline on the map. "I wish we could visit Alaska," he said. "I could take pictures and gather information as we traveled. But I know we can't go; it would cost too much money," David added, sounding grown up and wise.

"Yes, David," Mom sighed, "that would be a great vacation as well as a great learning experience! But I'm afraid you'll have to be satisfied with a trip to the library! Let's go after lunch."

Doing his research

"OK, Mom!" David grinned. He enjoyed going to the library.

David goes to school at home, and his mom is his teacher. As soon as Mother finished her housework, they went to the library to gather material on Alaska. David took a stack of books to the checkout desk.

"Wow! That's a lot of books!" the librarian said. "You must be doing a report."

David nodded. "Yes, on Alaska," he said. "I hope I can go there someday."

"Really?" The librarian nodded as she scanned each book. "Well, good luck on your report."

The next few days, David was busy reading the books on Alaska. Sometimes Mother sat with him and read the books with him. They talked about the pictures. The more David learned about Alaska, the more he wanted to go there.

"Mom, did you know that Alaska is twice the size of Texas?" David said one day. "But not many people live there because much of the state is covered with rugged mountains, and during winter with ice and snow. There aren't many roads into the interior, and if you want to go there, you have to fly!"

David studied about the native people who live in Alaska and learned that they live by fishing and hunting, just as their grandparents and great-grandparents had done for hundreds of years. The more he read about Alaska, the more he wanted to know.

An Alaskan birthday party

"I wish I could do something to help the people in Alaska learn about Jesus," David said one day. "Someday I may go there, but I want to do something now."

"Maybe you could raise some money and send it to a special project to help the people in Alaska," Mother suggested.

"I know!" David said excitedly. "My birthday is coming soon. I could have an Alaskan birthday party and tell my friends to bring money to tell people in Alaska about Jesus instead of buying gifts!"

"That's a wonderful idea!" Mom agreed. "We could write to friends and family members and invite them to help raise money for Alaska too."

David busily prepared for his party. He carved spears and canoes from wood and made tiny Eskimo parkas from leather.

Then David wrote a letter to family friends explaining that he wanted to help the people in Alaska learn about Jesus. Mother helped him, and soon he had a pile of letters to take to the post office. Imagine David's joy when letters began coming back with money inside. After his birthday David counted the money. He had two hundred forty dollars to send to Alaska to help the people learn about Jesus.

"Now how do we send the money?" David asked. "We don't know anyone in Alaska."

"Let's pray about it," Mother suggested. "I'm sure God will show us where He wants us to use this money."

A visitor from Alaska

A few days later, David dashed into the house out of breath and excited. "Guess what!" David said to his mom. "I just met Miss Beverly, a woman who lives in an Eskimo village in Alaska! She's visiting our neighbors. I'm going to talk to her later. Maybe she will know of a project that needs money."

Miss Beverly told David about summers when the sun never sets and described the beautiful lake and mountains she lived near. She told him about the Eskimos who were her neighbors. Then her eyes lighted up. She said, "I know just the place for your mission project! Near my home is a little Native American village called Togiak [*TOH-gee-ack*]. The little Seventh-day Adventist church there needs help. The church furnace doesn't work, and in the winter it gets very cold."

David listened carefully and tried to imagine what the church looked like. Beverly asked, "Would you like for your money to help repair the Togiak church?"

"Yes! That would be great!" David said. "Does the church have a pastor?"

"Yes," Miss Beverly said. "He flies into the village once a month or so. There are no roads that he can drive on, so he has to fly in. Lots of people in Togiak need to know about Jesus. If the church looked better, I think more people would come."

Raising money for Togiak

David nodded. "May I give you my two hundred forty dollars now?" David asked. "Then I'll get busy and raise some more money and send it to you. I want to help repair the church in Togiak so that many people can have a nice place to worship Jesus."

"Good!" Miss Beverly said. "I will give the money to the pastor and let you know what happens."

David got busy raising more money. He decided to have another birthday fund-raiser for his eleventh birthday. He wrote more letters to raise money for the Togiak church, and he mailed them to relatives, church members, and friends— just about everyone he and his mom could think of. Again money began coming in. By David's birthday he had four hundred dollars to send to Togiak. He was very excited.

Togiak church is repaired

Miss Beverly wrote David a letter saying that his gifts were enough to repair the Togiak church. "Now the church has a new metal roof, and we have painted it inside and out," she said. "Everyone in town comments about how nice the church looks! We also bought a new furnace so that people won't shiver in the church during the winter."

Miss Beverly's letters brought more good news. "Because the pastor cannot get to Togiak regularly, he has trained a couple to work with the people. They invited people to come to the church to see videos of Bible classes. Now more people are coming to the church every week. We hope soon many people in Togiak will learn to love Jesus!"

"Isn't that neat?" David said. "I'm glad that people in Alaska are learning about Jesus."

David's surprise project

Two months after David's eleventh birthday, he was busy doing his schoolwork when the telephone rang. Mother answered.

"David!" she called. "It's for you! Miss Beverly from Alaska wants to talk to you!"

David ran to the phone. "Hi!" he said. "This is David. What's up?"

"You know that we finished fixing the roof and putting in the furnace. But some other people heard about the church project and sent money for the furnace, so we didn't use all of your money. There is still some in the bank."

"What are you going to do with the money?" David asked.

"I have an idea," Miss Beverly said. "There is a family in town who is not Seventh-day Adventist, but the mother often brings the children to church. The children's names are Robert and Rochelle. Robert is ten, and Rochelle is eleven."

That's my age! David thought. *I wish I could meet them. It would be neat to meet some children who go to the church that I helped fix up in Togiak!*

Miss Beverly kept talking. "We'd like to send Robert and Rochelle to summer camp this summer. They can stay for a whole week and will have a good time learning about God, nature, and healthful living. But their family doesn't have the money for the camp fee. We thought maybe you would let us use the money that is left over from fixing the church to send Robert and Rochelle to summer camp. What would you think of that?"

"I've never been to summer camp," David said. "But I think it's a good idea for Robert and Rochelle to go. I want them to learn more about Jesus. Yes, you can use the money to send them to summer camp."

"Thank you, David," Miss Beverly said. "I know Robert and Rochelle will be really happy!"

Miss Beverly told Robert and Rochelle's mother the good news. The children were very excited! Robert and Rochelle loved summer camp. They loved the Bible stories, the crafts, and the songs. When they went back home, they told Miss Beverly and their family all they had learned. Now they go to church whenever they can.

Someday David hopes to meet Robert and Rochelle, perhaps when he at last gets to go to Alaska. But in the meantime, he's glad that God gave him the idea to help make a big difference to a small congregation in faraway Alaska.

Grandma's Radio Program

United States

Grandma had a radio program, and one day she had a surprise.

"Grandma is going to let us do it!" Nine-year-old Dorothy whispered excitedly to her two younger sisters. It was a dream come true, not only for Dorothy and her sisters but for their grandma too!

Grandma's dream

For years Grandma Boone has hosted a radio program every Sunday called *Your Bible Speaks*. During the program, Grandma reads from the Sabbath School lesson, plays songs, tells stories, prays, and wishes listeners a happy birthday. People from towns for miles around tune in to hear Grandma Boone talk about Jesus.

Dorothy has helped Grandma Boone with her radio program ever since she was little. One day Grandma suggested that the children might do a whole program by themselves. "Dorothy, you can be the host and announcer," Grandma explained. "Your sisters and some of your friends can play special music, read stories, read the prayer requests we receive, and give birthday greetings, just as I do," Grandma said.

Kids' radio program

The children liked the idea and practiced hard to make the program just right. They recorded the program ahead of time so there would be no mistakes when it was put on the radio. Finally the big day came. Dorothy and her sisters sat beside the radio, listening eagerly. It seemed funny to hear her own voice say, "Welcome to *Your Bible Speaks* radio program!"

"Hooray!" the children shouted.

As the children listened to the program, they wondered, *Will the people like it?* As the program ended, the telephones at the station started ringing. "That program was wonderful!" people said. "Who are those children?" "Will they do another program?" The station manager was surprised at how popular the program was. One person even teased Grandma that she did not need to do the program anymore; the children could do it!

Pint-size star

Several months later, the station manager talked to Grandma Boone about an idea he had. "Your children's program was so popular," he said. "I'd like to continue doing it. We have another half-hour time slot open on Sunday mornings. Do you think the children could produce a program every week?"

Dorothy could hardly believe it when Grandma Boone asked her, "How would you like to be a host, a real host, on your own radio program, just like mine?"

She thought for a moment and then said, "I think I could do it."

Suddenly there were so many things to do! The radio station paid for the first week of radio time, but after that Dorothy and her family had to raise seventy dollars each week to pay for the radio's air time. She asked local businesses to sponsor her program, and they did.

Then she had to plan a new program every week. Her sisters helped her by singing and announcing birthdays, and her little cousin recited Bible verses.

Just two days before the first broadcast, the town newspaper featured a large picture of Dorothy on the front page of the religion section. She was sitting at a desk, holding a script in one hand, and speaking into a microphone. The headline read, "A Show of Her Own." The story started out saying, "A nine-year-old girl is taking to the airwaves with her own Bible program."

Early on a spring Sunday morning, the first *Your Bible Speaks Children's Program* was broadcast over the airwaves and into thousands of listeners' homes. Dorothy's clear young voice welcomed the listeners and thanked Grandmother Boone for helping to make the program possible.

The little missionary

Can you name the people who were missionaries in this story? *(Grandmother Boone, Dorothy, her sisters, and the friends who helped with the radio program.)* They all shared their love for Jesus over the radio.

Dorothy was just nine years old when she started hosting her own radio program. She was being a missionary for Jesus. And her sisters were even younger. You are never too young to work for Jesus. And do not think that you need special talents to be a missionary for Jesus. Dorothy did not know she could host a radio program until she tried. And because she was willing to try, many people heard her tell about Jesus on Sunday mornings.

How can you be a missionary right now, right where you live?

Northern Asia-Pacific Division

Bonhang's Choice

South Korea

A young girl sets an example by choosing God over school and friends.

South Korea is a modern country, and people are free to become Christians if they wish. But freedom to believe does not always make it easy to be a Christian.

Bonhang's story

Bonhang *(boh-NANG)* started first grade in an Adventist school in South Korea. She went to classes Monday through Friday, but on Saturday she went to church. When she was eight years old, her family moved to a town where there was no Adventist school. So Bonhang enrolled in the public school.

Most government schools in South Korea hold classes from Monday through Saturday. Mother told Bonhang that she did not have to go to school on Saturday; she could attend Sabbath School on Sabbath and do her homework on Sunday. Bonhang was glad; she wanted to be in church with her parents on Sabbath.

On the first Friday of school, Bonhang told her teacher that she would not be in class on Saturday; she was going to church.

"But you must attend class every day," the teacher said.

"But Saturday is the day I worship God," Bonhang explained.

"Classes are dismissed at noon," the teacher said without smiling. "You can go to church in the afternoon."

Bonhang took her seat. She didn't know what to do. That evening Bonhang told her parents what the teacher had said. Mother explained that Adventists follow all of God's commandments and that makes them different from other Christians. And sometimes being different creates problems.

Problems

On Sabbath morning, Bonhang didn't go to school; she went to church with her parents. The following Monday the teacher asked Bonhang why she hadn't been in class on Saturday. *Why does she ask me that?* Bonhang wondered. *I told her I was going to go to church.*

Some of the children teased Bonhang about skipping classes; some called her lazy. Even the teacher made her feel bad that she was not at school on Saturday. Bonhang studied even harder, hoping to please her teacher.

The next Sabbath Bonhang again went to church.

After Sabbath, Bonhang called a classmate to ask for the assignments the teacher had given that day. But the girl said the teacher had not given any homework. Bonhang called another classmate, and she said the same thing. When Bonhang hung up the telephone, her mother asked her, "Did you get your assignments?"

"No," Bonhang answered. "My friends said there was no homework."

But on Monday morning the teacher stopped at Bonhang's desk and asked her, "Where is your homework?"

Bonhang told the teacher that she was told there were no assignments. The teacher told her that because she did not do the assignments, she would receive a zero for the day.

Bonhang's throat grew tight. She tried hard not to cry. *It isn't fair,* she thought to herself. *I would have done the homework if someone had told me the assignments.*

Try again

The next Sunday when Bonhang needed to get her assignments, Mother suggested that they go to visit her classmate's home and ask for the assignments in person. When they arrived, her friend was surprised to see her. When Bonhang asked her what the class did on Saturday, the girl told her that they finished the assignments in class, and there was no homework.

Bonhang asked her what assignments they did in class, but the girl said, "I don't remember." Finally Mother and Bonhang went home.

"Why is this happening?" Bonhang asked her mother. "What have I done to make them hate me?"

Mother visits the teacher

On Monday Mother visited the school to learn why the children would not give Bonhang the assignments. Mother was surprised when the teacher said, "I have told the children to not give assignments to anyone who skips classes on Saturdays."

The children continued to tease Bonhang for skipping

school on Saturdays. How would you feel if your friends teased you for doing what you knew was right?

Bonhang studied hard and received good grades in school in spite of the missed assignments.

The festival

One day the teacher announced that the school would have a special festival. It would include sports events and traditional Korean dancing. The children were excited about the festival. They practiced for the sporting events and tried out for the traditional dance program. Those who were chosen could wear beautiful Korean costumes.

To her surprise, Bonhang was chosen to be the lead in the traditional dances. She could hardly wait to tell her parents!

"When will the program be?" Mother asked Bonhang.

"The teacher did not say," Bonhang answered. "She will tell us later." Then Bonhang hurried to her room to practice her dance.

Several days later the teacher announced that the festival would be the following Saturday morning.

Saturday! Bonhang sat silently in her chair, but her heart cried out, *Why Saturday?*

Bonhang's choice

Bonhang's feet felt heavy as she walked home from school. Her mother asked if she was sick.

"No," Bonhang answered. "The teacher told us that the festival will be Saturday." Bonhang put her books down on the table and went to change her clothes.

Friday evening came. After worship, Bonhang's mother said, "Bonhang, it's your choice whether to go to the festival tomorrow or to church. Do what your heart tells you to do." Mother hugged Bonhang then left her alone.

That night Mother could not sleep. She went outside and looked into the star-filled sky. She prayed, "Father, Bonhang has worked so hard to prepare for the festival. Now she must choose between obeying You and attending the festival. Please comfort her. As young as she is, please help her to make the right choice."

Sabbath morning dawned bright and beautiful. The family gathered for worship and breakfast. Nobody mentioned the school festival, but Father and Mother were praying for Bonhang.

After breakfast Bonhang went to her room to dress. Mother wondered if Bonhang would choose her Sabbath dress or her lovely Korean costume. A few minutes later Bonhang came out of her room wearing her Sabbath dress and carrying her Bible. Mother felt a tear slip down her cheek. Even Father could not speak.

After church the family went for a walk in a beautiful park. Bonhang's parents hoped that it would help her to feel better about missing the festival. At sundown, Father led the family in worship to close the Sabbath. Then Mother asked Bonhang, "Are you sorry that you missed the festival?"

"I wanted to be in the festival," Bonhang answered. "But I wanted to spend Sabbath with you and Daddy and Jesus."

Telephone call

On Sunday morning the telephone rang. It was Bonhang's teacher. She asked Mother to come to the school on Monday. Mother wondered if the teacher would punish Bonhang for not attending the festival.

On Monday, Mother went to the school and found the teacher.

"I need to tell you," the teacher said, "that I have watched Bonhang for several months now. No matter how I punished her, she was determined to worship God on Saturday. Even when her classmates teased her, she did not give in.

"When I gave her the part in the festival, I was testing her. Bonhang practiced so hard that I was sure she would come to the festival." The teacher was smiling now. "But I decided to have another girl practice for the part, just in case Bonhang did not come."

Mother's eyes filled with tears as she listened to this teacher who had given her daughter so much trouble. The teacher took hold of Mother's hands. "I have never met such a sincere child as Bonhang. She may continue to worship on Saturday; I will not punish her anymore for missing classes."

Mother walked out of the school with a heart full of joy. "Thank You, Father," she whispered.

Bonhang had made a choice to be faithful to God. It was difficult, and people did not understand. But her faithfulness helped her classmates and her teacher see God's love in her life. Sometimes it is difficult to do what we know is right. But when we are faithful to God, He blesses us in ways we cannot imagine.

Run Away to Church

Taiwan

Sung sneaked away to church and brought her family with her.

Sung Yeon Yang *(Soong Yee-HWN Yang)* lives with her mother, father, and younger sister in the island of Taiwan, off the eastern coast of China. When Sung was little, her family worshiped Buddha. But then God led Sung to help her family learn about Jesus.

When Sung was in the first grade, her parents enrolled her in an English-language class after school. Even though learning English was difficult, Sung enjoyed it. The English-language class was sponsored by the Adventist church in her town.

One day Sung heard her teacher talking about the church's worship services on Saturday. Sung asked her teacher if she could attend the church too. The teacher told her she was welcome to come. That Saturday morning Sung slipped away from home and ran to the little church. She enjoyed the Sabbath School so much that she attended nearly every week.

Her parents thought she was taking part in a school activity, so they did not question where Sung was.

One day the teacher invited Sung to join the children's choir, which often sang for church. Sung loved to sing, and she eagerly joined the choir. This meant that at times she would have to stay for the church service so she could sing in the choir.

Don't tell Mother!

One week Sung invited her sister to go to church with her. "But don't tell Mother, and *don't* tell Father where we are going!" Sung warned. The sisters slipped away from home and ran to church. When church ended, the girls hurried home.

When they arrived home, Mother asked where they had gone. Usually when Mother had asked this question, Sung would make up a story so Mother and Father would not be angry. But this time Sung told the truth. "I have joined a children's choir at the Adventist church, and they sang today for worship," Sung said.

Mother was willing to let the girls go to church, but Father was not. "No, you may not go to any Christian church!" he told them. "We are Buddhists, and Buddhists do not attend Christian churches—even to sing in the choir." Mother felt bad that the girls could not go, so she allowed them to attend church when their father was not home. When Sung's father learned that the girls were still going to the church, he was angry at first. Then Mother explained that at church the girls had learned how to obey and be kind. She was sure attending church was helping them. Reluctantly Father allowed the girls to go to church.

Mother and Father visit

Six months later, Sung's mother met one of the church members in town. The woman invited her family to visit the church. Mother told Father that she thought it was time they go to the church and see what their daughters were learning. The girls were thrilled when their mother *and* father agreed to go to church with them on Sabbath.

Mother and Father found the church service very different from anything they had experienced before, and they were embarrassed and did not know what to do. But the members offered them songbooks and smiled at them. In spite of the members' efforts to be friendly, Mother and Father were not eager to return to the Christian church again. But Mother's friend kept inviting the family.

Come and pray

Then a woman from the church moved to their apartment building. Every morning she called the family and invited them to come to her apartment for worship. Sung's parents were pleased that someone cared enough about them to invite them to pray. For six months Sung's family went to the woman's house for prayer. Then Sung's mother suggested that the family begin having worship in their own apartment every morning. They had already learned how to worship and pray on their own.

Sung's father began reading the Bible with the pastor several times during the week. As he learned more about God and His love, he became more eager to worship the God of creation. He threw away his large collection of Buddhist books, he threw away his prayer beads, and he began praying from his heart. He went from being the leader of a

Buddhist home to being the spiritual leader of a Christian home.

Eighteen months after Sung ran away to church, her entire family became Adventist Christians. Father has become a gentler, happier man. Mother enjoys worshiping with the family, for she did not go to the Buddhist temple when Father went to pray. And Sung and her sister love to sing praises to Jesus in the children's choir. She is glad that she ran away to church.

South American Division

Curious Carla

Bolivia

As Carla passed the mud-brick building, she heard singing and stopped to listen.

Carla is ten years old. She lives in Bolivia, a beautiful country with tall mountains, high plains, and even rain forests. Carla lives on the Altiplano *(ahl-tee-PLAH-no)*, a large flat area high in the Andes Mountains.

What is it like to live on the Altiplano? If you have ever climbed a mountain, you know that the farther up you climb, the thinner the air becomes. And when the air is thin, you can get tired faster and have to stop to rest. It is warm when the sun shines, but when the sun goes behind clouds or when it sets behind the mountains in the evening, it gets cold fast. The people who live there carry blankets with them. Then if they get cold, they can wrap up in their blankets to keep warm.

Helping Mother

Carla has always lived on the Altiplano. She has never been to a big city or seen the ocean. But in many ways her life is like yours. She is in the fifth grade and enjoys science and math. She is a curious girl and likes to learn what makes things work.

When Carla is not in school, she often helps her mother sell biscuits and cookies at a little stand in the town's marketplace. Carla's father made her a flat wooden tray that she can use to carry some of her mother's cookies and biscuits. She walks along the street selling them to people. Carla likes to help her mother, and her mother is glad she is such a good helper.

Curious Carla

One Saturday morning as Carla walked down the road near her home, she passed by a little church. The door was open, and Carla could hear singing inside the building. She walked slowly past the door and tried to peek inside to see what was happening.

She saw children sitting on low benches and a woman standing in front of them. *I wonder what the children are doing in the church on Saturday?* Carla thought to herself as she continued walking down the dirt road. She wanted to stay and listen, but she was afraid that someone might yell at her for peeking into the church.

The sound of the children's voices made her want to know about what was happening inside the church. So a few minutes later, Carla walked slowly back up the hill and past the church's open door. This time she saw a woman talking to the children. The woman was holding a picture for the children to see. Carla wished she could see the picture, but the woman wasn't facing the door.

Several times Carla walked up the hill then back down the hill, pausing just outside the church door to hear and see what was going on inside. She wished that she could go inside and sit down and listen with the other children. But she had not been invited, and she did not want to get into trouble.

Discovered

But someone had seen Carla at the doorway. The woman watched as Carla walked back and forth past the doorway, looking in each time. Quietly the woman went to the doorway. When Carla neared the church door once more, the woman stepped out to talk to her. "Would you like to come in and join the children?" the woman asked.

Carla looked at the woman's smiling face and decided that it was OK to go into the church now that the woman had invited her. She sat down on the bench with the other children and listened as the teacher told a story about Moses. Then the children sang some songs about Jesus. Carla had never been inside a church before, so the songs and the stories were new to her. But she liked it.

After church Carla hurried home and told her mother where she had been. She repeated the Bible story she had heard. Then she asked, "Mother, may I go to church again next Saturday? The woman said I could come." Mother said it was OK.

The next Saturday Carla returned to the little church. This time she did not stand at the door and listen. She walked in and sat down. She listened to the stories and tried to sing along with the children.

When Carla arrived home, she told her mother what she had learned. Carla's little sister, Janet, heard what she said and wanted to go to Sabbath School too. "May I take Janet next week?" Carla asked. Mother agreed.

Janet did go to church with Carla, and she liked Sabbath School too. After that the two girls went to church together every week.

For four months Janet and Carla went to the little Adventist church. Every week they told their mother the stories they had heard and sang the songs that they had learned. Mother liked to hear her girls sing the happy songs. And every week they asked Mother to help them learn their Bible verse so they could get a star by their name on the chart at church.

Please come!

One day the pastor urged everyone to invite their friends and family members to come to some special meetings at the church. Carla hurried home and invited her mother to go to church with her. Mother agreed and began attending church with the girls. Soon Father began attending church with the family too. Father and Mother began studying the Bible with a member of the church so they could know more about God.

"I am glad that I was curious when I heard the children singing through the open church door," Carla says. "I am happy that the teacher invited me in. Now I love Jesus, and I want everyone to love Him." Carla has another piece of advice for us. "Don't be afraid to invite your friends to church. You might be surprised which of your friends would enjoy Sabbath School too."

Carla has invited some of her school friends and her cousins to church. Some of them have come to church with her. Carla is doing just what Jesus wants her to do. She is being a missionary. Let's pray that Carla—and all the children in the Seventh-day Adventist church in her town in Bolivia—will continue to be missionaries for Jesus.

Mission Under the Mango Tree

Brazil

Eric Monnier*

Marcos wanted a star in his crown, but he didn't know how to lead someone to Jesus.

Marcos *(MAHR-cohs)* sat under his favorite mango tree. He often sat here when he had some important thinking to do. The pastor had said in the sermon that day that everyone who goes to heaven will have a star in their crown for each person they helped to love Jesus. *What can I do to help someone to know Jesus?* Marcos wondered. *I want to have a star in my crown when Jesus takes me to heaven.*

Marcos remembered that the pastor said that some people hold branch Sabbath Schools, but Marcos did not know how to hold a branch Sabbath School. The pastor said some people preach, and others tell their friends about Jesus. But Marcos did not know how to preach, and he wasn't sure how to tell his friends about Jesus.

---

* Eric Monnier is president of the Bolivian Union.

Marcos pulled his old harmonica out of his pocket, leaned against the tree trunk, and began playing a Sabbath song to help him think better. He loved music, and although he had never had a music lesson, he had taught himself to play a few of his favorite songs. As he played, Marcos wondered if God could help him use his harmonica to tell someone about Jesus.

"That sounds nice." The voice startled Marcos, who stopped playing and looked up. A neighbor boy stood nearby. "You play well," the boy said.

"Thanks!" Marcos said, excited, for suddenly he had an idea. "Do you want to learn to sing that song? I can teach you the words, and then we can sing and play it together!"

"Sure," the boy said. He sat down beside Marcos and listened to the melody as Marcos played the song again.

"Now I'll sing the words, and you join in when you can," Marcos said. He began singing "Jesus Loves Me." Soon the boy could sing along with Marcos. While they were singing, some other boys stopped and listened.

"Do you want to learn the song too?" he asked the boys. Some of the boys nodded, and others said Yes. Marcos began singing the song again, this time with the help of his friend. Soon the others were joining in too.

When the boys knew the song, Marcos played his harmonica while they sang. Then he thought, *This is like a branch Sabbath School. I should preach a sermon, but I don't know one.* Then he had an idea. He could tell the boys the Bible story he had studied in Sabbath School that day.

"Do you want me to tell you a story?" he asked the neighbor boys.

"Sure!" "Yes." "OK," they answered, and everyone sat down under the mango tree to listen. Marcos tried hard to tell the story just as he had read it in his lesson. When he finished, one of the boys asked for another story. "Yes, tell us another," a second boy said. "Go ahead, tell us more stories," another boy said.

Marcos thought for a moment and then told the boys another favorite Bible story. "Once there was a young boy named David. He was very brave," Marcos began.

Suddenly Marcos had an idea. "If you would like to hear more stories, come back next Saturday afternoon, and I will teach you more songs and tell you another story."

Marcos's branch Sabbath School

The children agreed to return the following week to hear more stories.

The next Sabbath in church, Marcos listened very carefully as the teacher told the Bible lesson. He wanted to remember every bit of it so he could repeat it to his friends that afternoon.

After church Marcos hurried home and walked to his mango tree. Would the children remember to come? Sure enough, several children sat waiting for him. Some had brought their friends who wanted to hear the stories Marcos told.

Week after week Marcos studied his lesson, memorized the words to songs and Bible texts, and hurried home to meet the boys and girls who waited for him under the mango tree. Soon up to twenty children joined him on Sabbath afternoon for Bible stories and songs.

Marcos realized that soon he would have told all the stories he knew. How could he learn new ones quickly enough to tell his friends? Then he had an idea. "I don't tell the stories as well as my teacher at church does," Marcos explained. "I would like you to hear her tell the stories. Would you like to come with me to Sabbath School next Saturday and hear my teacher tell the stories? We sing these same songs there too." The children nodded. "Be here next Saturday morning at nine o'clock then," Marcos said before his friends went home. "I will take you to my Sabbath School. You'll like my teacher. She is a really good storyteller."

All week Marcos wondered whether his friends would come to the mango tree on Sabbath morning. Would they be willing to go into the church to learn more about God? On Sabbath morning Marcos dressed for church and waited under the mango tree for his friends. He did not have to wait long. Soon several children stood with him under the mango tree. They wanted to go to church and hear more Bible stories.

The mango-tree gang

That morning when Marcos walked into Sabbath School, twenty of his friends followed him. His Sabbath School teacher looked at all the visitors. She had never seen so many new children in Sabbath School.

"Welcome to Sabbath School!" she said. "Where did all our visitors come from?"

"Marcos invited us," one girl said. "We are his mango-tree gang," another said.

"Marcos tells us stories and teaches us songs," a third child added. "Marcos said that if we come with him to Sabbath School, you will teach us more songs and tell us more stories." The other children nodded.

"I told them you are a better teacher than I am," Marcos added quietly.

The children loved the stories and songs they learned in Sabbath School. Many came back week after week. Marcos's teacher asked him how he had convinced so many children to come to Sabbath School.

"Remember when the pastor told us about having our own mission project and leading people to Jesus so we can have stars in our crown?" Marcos asked. "I did not know what I could do to lead someone to Jesus, so I asked Jesus to help me find something to do. I sat down and started playing my harmonica, and all these kids came by to listen. Then I told them a story, and they wanted to hear more. So I guess this is my mission project."

Marcos's friends continued coming to Sabbath School. Some invited their parents to attend church with them. And some of the parents asked the pastor to study the Bible with them and teach them about Jesus. Several months later there was a baptism. When the pastor asked each candidate to say how he or she began to attend church, six persons said that Marcos's mission under the mango tree had first introduced them to Jesus.

Marcos smiled broadly. *Now,* he thought, *when Jesus gives me my crown, there will be stars in it!*

South Pacific Division

Louisa's Lunch

Papua New Guinea

Louisa was amazed at the change in Joey, all because of a little kindness.

Louisa lived in Lae *(lay)*, a city in Papua New Guinea. She loved school, and she had lots of friends.

Naughty Joey

But there was one boy in her class that Louisa did not want to make friends with. No one liked Joey. He was a bully. He was bigger than the other children, and he was rude. When the children were playing, Joey often ran into them. Sometimes he knocked them over, but he never helped them get up; he never told them he was sorry. If a child walked past Joey in class, Joey sometimes stuck out his foot to trip the other child. Sometimes the child would fall down.

But the thing that made the other children dislike Joey the most was when he would grab another child's lunch and run away to eat it. Sometimes Joey took Louisa's lunch, too, but she did not tell her mother. She was afraid that Joey would be angry with her and hurt her.

The teacher never seemed to see Joey give the children a hard time. No one reported Joey's misbehavior because they all were afraid of what Joey might do to them. Joey made life unhappy for all the children in his class.

Tears

One afternoon as Louisa was walking out of class, Joey stuck out his foot and tripped her. Louisa fell flat on her face. It hurt, and Louisa started crying. But Joey did not help her up. He did not tell her he was sorry. Joey just ran away. Louisa stood up, picked up her papers, and walked to where her mother was waiting.

Mother saw tears in Louisa's eyes and asked, "What happened to you? Why are you crying?"

Louisa did not want to tell her mother that Joey had made her fall down. She did not want her mother to tell the teacher that Joey had hurt her. But mothers know when something is wrong, and Louisa's mother kept asking Louisa what had happened to make her cry. Finally Louisa told her that Joey had tripped her and made her fall. Mother listened quietly, and then she asked, "Is this the first time Joey has done this to you?"

"No," Louisa admitted. Then she told her mother that Joey was mean to all the children in class. "He punches us and trips us and takes our lunches and eats them. He's so mean!" Louisa felt tears sting her eyes.

"I think I have an idea how we can handle Joey," Mother said. Louisa wondered what her mother's plan was. *Will she tell the teacher? Will she tell Joey's mother? Will Joey get mad and hit me?*

Mother's plan

The next morning Louisa did not want to go to school. She did not want to face Joey again. But Mother encouraged her to eat her breakfast. Then she gave Louisa two lunches. "What is this for?" Louisa asked, holding up the extra sack lunch.

"That's for Joey," Mother said.

For Joey! Louisa wondered if Mother knew what she was doing.

"Take it," Mother said. "Give it to Joey. You might be surprised at what happens." Mother's smile gave Louisa the courage to take the lunch.

When Louisa arrived at school, Joey was already there. Louisa did not wait for Joey to take her lunch. She walked up to his desk and handed him the sack.

"What is this?" Joey asked.

"It's for you," Louisa said. "It's your lunch."

Joey took the sack and opened it. He saw a sandwich and a banana inside and some cookies. He did not say anything to Louisa but quietly walked away. Louisa thought she saw tears in Joey's eyes. A few minutes later Joey came back without the lunch.

"Thank you for the lunch," Joey said quietly to Louisa. Then he added something that surprised Louisa. "From now on, if anyone tries to hurt you, just let me know. I'll protect you." Louisa learned that Joey's family was poor. He usually came to school hungry. Then Louisa realized why Joey took the children's lunches.

Louisa had been afraid of Joey, but her little act of kindness had changed him.

That afternoon Louisa told her mother what had happened. "How did you know that Joey was hungry, Mom?" she asked.

"Sometimes when people are mean, it's because they need a little kindness. If we treat others with kindness, they will be kind in return."

Louisa never forgot the lesson she learned that day. And she never had any more trouble from Joey.

The Red Motorbike

Papua New Guinea

Maye Porter*

God uses lots of ways—even a red motorbike—to lead people to Jesus.

Eleven-year-old Aloyis *(ah-LOYS)* lives in a little village on the island of New Ireland, part of Papua New Guinea. The village sits near the main road that runs the length of the island.

The motorbike

One morning Aloyis heard the *vroom, vroom, vroom* of a motorbike. He ran to the road in time to see a red motorbike roar past. That evening Aloyis heard the motorbike roar past again. *I wonder where that man has been,* Aloyis thought.

The next day Aloyis heard the motorbike again. For several days it passed his home every morning and again every

---

* Maye Porter and her pastor-husband, George, have served as missionaries in the South Pacific, including Cook Islands, Fiji, and Papua New Guinea. They now share their faith on Norfolk Island, off the coast of eastern Australia.

evening. *What is going on?* Aloyis wondered. He decided to find out.

Early the next morning, Aloyis started down the road in the direction the man on the motorbike would be going. Soon he heard *vroom, vroom, vroom* behind him. He stepped off the road and watched the man and motorbike whiz past.

I bet he's going to the next village! Aloyis thought, and he ran down the road toward the next village.

The bamboo church

Sure enough, when Aloyis arrived in the next village, he saw the red motorbike parked under a tree. Nearby was a half-completed building made of bamboo. Aloyis saw one of his friends nearby and asked him, "What are they building?"

"A church," his friend answered.

"Who owns the red motorbike?" Aloyis asked.

"That's Pastor Maisi *(MY-see),*" his friend said, pointing to a man working on the church. "He's the pastor of the new church."

Aloyis walked over to the pastor and asked, "May I help?"

"Sure," Pastor Maisi said. "We need help thatching the roof."

At lunchtime someone gave Aloyis a plate of food to eat. Pastor Maisi brought his plate of food over to where Aloyis was eating and squatted down nearby. "You are a good worker!" he said.

Another man who had been working on the church stopped under the tree to eat. "Do you think the church will be ready in time for worship this Sabbath?" he asked.

"If we keep working as hard as we have been, it should be done before Sabbath," the pastor answered, smiling.

"Sabbath?" Aloyis asked his friend. "What is Sabbath?"

"Saturday," his friend answered.

Aloyis decided to attend the church meeting on Saturday. After all, he had helped build the church, and that way he could see Pastor Maisi—and his red motorbike—again.

Aloyis goes to church

On Sabbath morning, Aloyis awoke early and jumped out of bed. He dressed in his everyday clothes and put his best shirt and shorts into a bag. Then he set off down the path that led to the church in the next village.

I wonder what the meeting will be like, Aloyis thought as he hurried along the path. *I think it will be great because Pastor Maisi is such a nice man.*

Aloyis stopped at a creek near the village and washed the dust off his arms and face and legs. Then he changed into his good clothes and stuffed the old clothes into the bag. He hurried to the church. He was the first one there!

Sabbath School begins

The new bamboo walls smelled fresh and good. He looked around at the neat building. *I helped build this!* he thought. *Pastor Maisi said I was a good worker.*

Soon Aloyis heard the *vroom, vroom, vroom* of the red motorbike as it cruised into the village. He ran outside to greet the pastor.

"Hello there!" Pastor Maisi called, smiling at Aloyis. "I'm glad you came to Sabbath School!"

People heard the pastor's motorbike and walked toward the church. Soon the church was full. The people sang many songs that Aloyis did not know. He listened carefully, and soon he could sing along. He loved the Bible stories and found Pastor Maisi's sermon interesting.

After the meeting everyone shared a big lunch.

"Come back next week," Pastor Maisi told Aloyis when the afternoon program ended.

"I will!" Aloyis promised.

Aloyis started toward home. Outside the village he stopped to change into his old clothes before he hurried home. He slipped into the house without his parents' seeing him. He was not sure they would want him going to church, and he did not want them to stop him from seeing his new friend, Pastor Maisi.

The next Sabbath Aloyis got up early again, dressed in his old clothes, and ran along the dirt path to the next village. Once again he stopped to wash and change into his good clothes before going to church. When the meeting was over, he changed clothes and ran back home. No one seemed to notice that he'd been gone.

Caught!

The next week Aloyis again went to church. He had such a wonderful time! As he walked home he thought about the stories Pastor Maisi had told. He was so busy thinking that he forgot to change his clothes. He walked into his house wearing his good shorts and shirt.

"Where have you been in your good clothes?" his mother asked. Aloyis looked at his shirt. He told his mother that he had been to church.

"I don't want you going to that Saturday church!" his mother said.

Aloyis did not answer. He still wanted to go to church. That week he was extra helpful at home, and he told his parents what he had learned in the church. On Sabbath his mother let him go to Sabbath School.

Aloyis's parents noticed that Aloyis was changing. He had become more obedient, kind, and helpful. His parents asked Aloyis to ask Pastor Maisi to visit them. When he came, they asked him to teach them the Bible. Before long others in the village began to study the Bible with Pastor Maisi. Soon there were enough people in Aloyis's village to have a church of their own. Today Aloysis no longer has to run to the next village to attend church. He and his parents walk to Sabbath School in their own village.

Southern Africa–Indian Ocean Division

The Boy Who Refused to Pray

Madagascar

When we worship God, we honor Him and help others want to know Him better too.

Israel is six years old. He lives on the island of Madagascar (*mah-dah-GAHS-car*), off the eastern coast of Africa. Israel's family is Adventist, but there is no Adventist school where he lives. His family decided to send him to a school sponsored by another church rather than to a public school.

Israel liked school; and he especially liked his teacher, a nice young woman with a soft voice and gentle manner. He was quick to raise his hand when the teacher asked a question or needed a volunteer. But when the children prayed, Israel remained quiet. He bowed his head with the other children, but when the teacher said a prayer for the children to repeat, Israel did not join in.

Israel was a happy, obedient boy in every other way. So the teacher was surprised that he refused to pray with the other children. One day she asked him, "Israel, I've noticed that when the children bow their heads to pray, you do not repeat the prayer with them. Why is this?"

Israel answered simply, "At home we pray in a different way."

"How is that?" the teacher asked.

"We don't memorize a prayer and pray it every day," he explained. "We tell Jesus what is in our hearts, just as we would talk to a friend."

"Would you like to lead the children in their prayer tomorrow?" Israel's teacher asked.

"Yes." Israel smiled. "I would like that."

"By the way," the teacher added, "what church do you attend?"

"We are Seventh-day Adventists," Israel said.

Prayer time

The next day when it was time for prayer, the teacher asked Israel to lead the children in the prayer. Everyone bowed their heads and folded their hands. Israel stood and prayed a simple prayer, "Lord Jesus, thank You for our food. Please bless us all. Amen."

Some of the children giggled. "Teacher," one child said, "Israel did not cross himself."

"And he did not add 'in the name of the Father, the Son, and the Holy Ghost' either," another boy pointed out.

Later the teacher quietly asked Israel why he had not led the children in the prayer she had taught them. "I prayed the way we pray at home," he said. "We say what we feel in our heart, not what we have memorized. And we don't cross ourselves when we pray."

"Oh," the teacher said, surprised.

Trouble with tests

It was time for midyear exams. Israel's teacher realized that Israel would have problems on the religion exam, during which the children were required to recite prayers that they had learned during the term. Her supervisor told her that if Israel refused to recite the prayers as required, he would receive a zero on his exam. But the teacher did not want to fail this sweet child. She decided to visit his parents. Perhaps they could help Israel learn the prayers.

Israel's parents listened politely as their son's teacher explained her concerns. They told her that Israel knew the prayers she had taught and could recite them for the exam, but those prayers meant nothing to him in his personal life; they were not the kind of prayers they prayed at home or at church.

Then Israel's mother gave the teacher a book to read. "Perhaps this book will help you understand why we pray as we do," she said. The teacher thanked her and took the book home, promising to read it.

As the teacher read the book, she began to understand what this boy and his family believed and why he prayed as he did. She discovered other truths that she had not heard before. *Why did we not learn these things in our religious studies?* she wondered.

A request

Several weeks later the teacher went to visit Israel's parents again. "I have been reading the book you gave me," she said, "and I was wondering if you would answer some questions." Israel's mother smiled. The two studied for a long time, and before the teacher left, she asked Israel's parents to pray for her. They promised to pray every day.

At the end of the school year, Israel's teacher stopped teaching at the religious school. She stopped attending the church she had grown up in. Now she attends church with Israel's family, all because one little boy refused to pray as she had taught him.

Israel was right. If we are faithful to do what we know is right, we, too, can make a difference in someone else's life. Let's ask Jesus to help us make a difference this week.

Under the Mopane Tree

Namibia

Gideon and Pam Peterson*

Our story today comes from the country of Namibia *(nah-MIH-bee-ah)* in southwestern Africa. Usually land that lies along an ocean is green and fertile. But in Namibia, the land along the ocean is one of the driest deserts in the world.

Northwestern Namibia gets a little more rain, and a few trees and shrubs can grow, but still it is very dry. This is the land of the Himba people. They raise cattle, sheep, and goats. When there is no rain, there is no food for the animals, and the people must take their herds to another area to graze. Because the Himba move often, they build simple houses made of mud and thatch to live in.

Wauta

Wauta *(wah-OO-tah)* is a Himba boy. His family lives on the edge of the great Namib Desert. The children in Wauta's

---

* Gideon and Pam Peterson are missionaries among the Himba people of Namibia.

settlement do not go to school. The boys help care for the cattle, and the girls help their mothers carry water, prepare meals, and care for the baby goats and sheep.

Wauta was about six years old when a missionary couple, Mr. and Mrs. Peterson, visited his village. Wauta loved the stories they told, and whenever he saw the cloud of dust that their old pickup kicked up, he ran to greet them. Then he called the other children to come to the mopane *(moh-PAH-nee)* tree to hear stories about Jesus. Wauta made it his job to see that the children—even ones older than he was—stayed quiet while Mr. Peterson talked.

Where is Wauta?

One week Wauta was not waiting for the missionaries. "Where is Wauta?" they asked. His mother said that he had gone to help his brothers care for their cattle.

Later the missionaries learned that Wauta's mother was ill. They stopped to visit her. "I'm so glad you came," she said. "The doctors can do nothing to help me, but Wauta says that your prayers will heal me." The missionaries prayed for her, and the next time they visited, she was feeling better.

The mopane-tree church

The Himba people do not have a church in which to worship. They meet under the mopane tree, which is the biggest tree in the area. The tree shades the people from the hot African sun. Since it seldom rains, they do not need a roof.

Even though the people do not worship in a church, their place of worship under the tree is special to them. In one settlement the children decided to make their tree-church more beautiful. They cleared the area of branches and rocks and swept away all the leaves and twigs. Then they gathered large stones and laid them neatly in a large circle, outlining what they thought should be the church's boundary. Then the children waited eagerly to show the missionaries their beautiful church.

The mopane-tree school

Because the children must help their parents care for their family's animals and help prepare food, they cannot go to school. Imagine the excitement when the children learned that the missionaries were going to hold a school for them under the mopane tree! When it was time for school to start, someone honked the horn in the missionary's truck, and children came running from all directions. The slowest child had to remain behind with the animals while the others went to school.

The children learned to write by using sticks to make letters in the dirt. Then some children in South Africa learned about the Himba school under the mopane tree. They wanted to help these children learn to read and write, so they donated notebooks to write in. The missionaries bought pencils, and soon the children learned to write in their notebooks. Mr. Peterson translated Bible stories into their language and began teaching the children how to read them. The children were so excited to have a book in their own language!

Others want to come

The mopane-tree church and school is not far from another village, and the children of this village wanted to learn about Jesus too. They begged the missionaries to wait to start teaching until they could run to the mopane tree, so they would not miss anything. Sometimes the missionaries found the children waiting near the road when they passed. Then the missionaries stopped and picked them up on the way to the mopane-tree school.

The Himba children of northern Namibia are just beginning to learn about Jesus. Let's pray that God will make a way that they will soon give their hearts to God and that their parents will want to learn more about Jesus, as well.

Southern Asia
Division

No Longer Bored

India

Jean Sundaram*

Have you ever been bored on Sabbath? Maybe these two boys' ideas will help you find something special to do.

"I'm bored!" Davidson told his brother one Sabbath after lunch. He did not feel like reading, but he could not think of anything else to do.

"I know," said his brother, Samuelson. "Let's walk to the next village. Maybe we will find something interesting along the way." The two boys told their parents of their plans and set off toward the next village, three miles (five kilometers) away.

"This is better than sitting around doing nothing," Davidson said as they walked along the dusty road.

Who are you?

When they reached the next village, they sat down under

---

* Jean Sundaram is Shepherdess coordinator and women's ministries director in the South India Union.

the shade of a big tree to rest. Soon some children noticed the boys and came over to where they were sitting.

"What is your name?" one boy asked. "Where are you from?" another asked.

"I'm Samuelson, and this is my brother Davidson," Samuelson said. "We live in the next village and attend Thomas Memorial School. Have you heard of it?"

Some of the children nodded. "What is the school like?" one of the children asked.

"Oh, it is pretty nice," Davidson said. "We study math and reading and English and all that, but we also learn about Jesus in our morals classes, and we sing nice songs." Then Davidson had an idea. "Would you like to learn a song? We can teach you one."

"Yes! Yes!" the children chorused. "Teach us a song."

Samuelson and Davidson taught them a Christian song, and soon the children were singing along. "Teach us another song," one of the children said. So the boys taught the children another song.

Then one of the children said, "Tell us a story. We like stories."

Davidson looked at Samuelson. "You tell a story," he said. "You can do better than I. Tell the one that we studied in our lesson today. I'll help you if you get stuck."

So the boys told the children a story about Jesus.

"We liked that story," the children said. "Tell us another one."

Time to leave

Samuelson looked at the sun hanging low in the sky. "It's getting late," he said. "We have to leave now. But maybe we can come next week and teach you some more songs and tell you some more stories. OK?"

The children agreed. They followed the brothers down the dusty road. "Don't forget to come back next week," the children reminded them.

The next Sabbath, Samuelson and Davidson returned to the neighboring village. When they arrived, the children came running to greet them. They sat down under the big tree, ready to sing and hear more stories. Several old men and women of the village came and sat on the ground with the children and listened.

"We have a program at our school every Saturday morning," Samuelson said. "Our teachers tell stories better than we can. If you come to our school next Saturday morning, you can hear more stories and sing more songs."

Visitors

On Sabbath morning, the teachers were surprised to see thirty children from the village walking toward the church on campus. Davidson and Samuelson took the children to their Sabbath School class, where they had a wonderful time learning more about Jesus.

That afternoon Davidson and Samuelson decided that they should start a branch Sabbath School in the village. They found some teachers and other students who could help them.

Samuelson, Davidson, and the other students and teachers visited the homes of the children and talked with their parents. They prayed for those who were sick and invited the parents to come to the branch Sabbath School meetings for the adults.

No longer bored

"We are not bored on Sabbath any longer," Davidson says. "We are too busy teaching our new friends about Jesus. It is a lot of fun to work for Jesus like this!"

Today seventy people attend the branch Sabbath School in the village. Soon some of them will be baptized. They need a church to worship in so they can continue to invite their families and friends to meet their friend Jesus.

Promila and the Runaway Goats

India

C. Aitawna*

Did you know that even goats can help people want to learn about Jesus?

"Promila *(pro-MEE-lah)*, Father is coming," Mother called. "Come see what he has brought!"

Six-year-old Promila peeked out the door of the family's tiny bamboo house. Her eyes grew wide as she saw her father and the pastor bringing five little goats into the yard. She was not sure whether the goats would bite her, so she stayed safely in the house, which is built on stilts.

"It's OK," her mother said. "The goats won't hurt you. Come and help Father put them into the pen he has made." Promila started down the ramp that led to the ground. Soon she was helping her brother and sister chase the goats into the pen. "The goats will stay with us over the Sabbath," Father said. "On Sunday the pastor will take them to their new owners in the village. The goats are a gift from

* C. Aitawna, now retired, was director of the Arunachal Pradesh region, Pasighat, Arunachal Pradesh, India, when he shared this story.

ADRA and will help the people in the village earn money."

The children played with the goats until Mother called them to come in. It was almost sunset and time for worship. As the sun slid behind the jungle trees, some villagers joined the family for worship. Soon sounds of happy singing filled the little clearing in the jungle as the people welcomed the Sabbath. Promila was glad that she and her family were Christians. She loved to listen to the stories the pastor told them about Jesus.

Runaway goats

Sabbath was a happy day. The believers again gathered in Promila's little house for Bible study, prayer, and worship. After the afternoon meeting ended, the children ran outside to visit the goats. But the goat pen was empty. Then the children saw a hole in the pen.

"Daddy! Daddy! The goats are gone!" Promila yelled as she ran up the ramp and into the house. "The goats have run away!" she cried.

Everyone went outside to look for the goats. They searched around the house and under the house, but the goats were not there. They searched behind the bushes and in the rice fields, but the goats were not there either. Some of the men began looking in the jungle near Promila's house, but the sun was setting, and they had to stop. It would soon be dark, and the jungle is dangerous at night.

"We have to find the goats!" Promila cried. "We can't let the wild animals eat them! Please, Daddy, we must look for them!"

"No," Father said. "It is not safe for us in the jungle now either."

Then the pastor made a suggestion. "We can pray and ask God to protect the goats until we can find them in the morning. Come, let's kneel and ask God to send angels to keep the lost goats safe through the night."

As the grown-ups prayed, Promila whispered her own prayer. "Please, Jesus, You can do anything. Please send angels to keep the goats safe."

That night Promila could not sleep. She lay on her mat thinking about the goats. She imagined tigers stalking them. But then she remembered that God's angels were watching over the goats. They would send the tigers away. Finally Promila slept.

Looking for the goats

Early the next morning, the pastor and Promila's father set out on the jungle path toward the village they had passed through on Friday when they brought the goats to Promila's home. Just before they reached the village, they saw some men walking toward them with five little goats!

"These must be your goats," one man said. "They came running down the jungle path last night just before dark. We are bringing them back to you."

"Thank you so much!" Promila's father said. "We asked Jesus to send angels to watch over our goats, and He sent you!"

People in the village soon heard about how God had protected the goats. They began asking questions about the Christians' powerful God. And now many more people crowd into Promila's home on Sabbath to learn more about Jesus and how they can become His followers too.

Southern Asia–Pacific Division

Take Me With You!

Philippines

When you read about Marlo, you learn that kids of any age can work for Jesus.

Marlo is eleven years old. He lives with his older brother, Rodrigo *(roh-DREE-goh)*, and little sister, Sandra, in a city with a pretty name—Iloilo *(EE-lo-EE-lo)*. Iloilo is a seaport city in central Philippines. Marlo's father works on a large ship. He is away from home for weeks at a time. Marlo's mother died when little Sandra was born, so Marlo, Rodrigo, and Sandra live with their grandmother.

Marlo's family is not Seventh-day Adventist, but Marlo and Rodrigo attend a Seventh-day Adventist elementary school.

Rodrigo goes to church

One day Joey, a boy in Rodrigo's class, invited Rodrigo to go to the Adventist church. Rodrigo did not know what to tell his friend. He was not sure that his grandmother would let him go. Joey kept inviting Rodrigo to church, so finally Rodrigo agreed to ask his grandmother. Rodrigo was surprised when she said Yes.

Rodrigo wondered if he would be bored in church, but he was surprised to find that he really enjoyed the service! It was different from the church his grandmother attended. The following week when Joey asked him to go, Rodrigo accepted. Soon he was attending church every week.

Take me with you!

Marlo wanted to go to church with Rodrigo. Rodrigo told his younger brother that he did not think Marlo could sit still through Sabbath School and church. But Marlo did not give up. Every week he begged, "Please, Rodrigo, take me with you!" Finally Rodrigo agreed to take Marlo. "You'd better be quiet," Rodrigo warned his brother with a smile.

Marlo liked Sabbath School, especially when the children shook his hand during the welcome song. Marlo knew some of the songs the children sang, for he had sung them at school. Soon he was singing along.

Children's meetings

At school, Marlo's teacher announced that there would be citywide Bible lectures, and the children would help—not just take up the offering and hand out cards. The children would preach, present the special music, read Scripture, usher—everything. Rodrigo and Marlo signed up to sing in the choir, and Rodrigo's friend Joey preached.

Rodrigo and Marlo's father came home during the meetings. Marlo was very glad to see his dad. He invited his dad to come to the meetings to hear Rodrigo and him sing. Their father took them to the meetings, but he decided to wait for the boys outside. He could still hear the children preaching from where he waited.

Every night the speaker made an altar call. One evening early in the series of meetings, Rodrigo decided to be baptized. Soon Marlo joined him. They began Bible studies to prepare for baptism. Marlo was one of the youngest ones in the class, but he studied faithfully and knew the answers to the questions every week.

The children had to get their parents' permission to be baptized. Rodrigo and Marlo were sure that their grandmother would not give them permission, so they asked their father. To their surprise, their father gave the boys permission to be baptized.

Too young?

The church board voted on the names of the children who had prepared for baptism. But when Marlo's name came up, some people felt that because his parents were not Adventist, he was too young to be baptized. Marlo was very disappointed when the pastor told him. "But I have studied all the Bible lessons, and my father has given his permission. I want to be baptized." The pastor smiled and told Marlo that he would see what he could do.

The pastor asked Marlo's teachers for advice. "If you think that Marlo is ready for baptism, I will go back to the church board and ask them to reconsider." The teachers told him that Marlo has an honest heart. They promised to be Marlo's spiritual guardians.

The pastor told the church board what the teachers had said and asked them to reconsider their decision. This time the board members were happy to recommend that Marlo be baptized.

Marlo was the youngest one to be baptized that day. But already he finds ways to serve God. When visitors come to his Sabbath School, Marlo always shakes their hands and makes them feel welcome, just as others made him feel welcome when he first came.

We are never too young to follow Jesus. And even if we are not a baptized member of the church, we can work for Jesus. How many ways can you think of to work for Jesus right now?

A Shining Star for Jesus

Myanmar

When one girl in a little village learned of God's love, she could not keep the good news to herself.

Thiridon *(THEE-ree-dawn)* is an eleven-year-old girl who lives in southern Myanmar. Most of the people in Myanmar worship golden idols. They bring gifts of incense and flowers to lay at the idol's feet. Then they kneel down and pray.

Thiridon lives in a small village in the countryside. Most of the villagers are farmers. They live in small houses of one or two rooms. Mostly the houses are made of bamboo and have thatched roofs. The villagers do not have cars to ride in or books to read in their homes. In fact, when Thiridon was little, the village did not even have a school.

God opens the way

Thiridon is a bright girl. From the time she was little, she begged her parents to let her go to school. The nearest school was in the next village. Then some Adventist Christians began working and praying to build a little church school for the children. Relatives of some of the villagers learned about the need for a school and helped build one. Now the children can attend school in their own village.

When the school first opened, the children sat on rough bamboo benches, but they did not mind. They were glad that they had a school where they could learn!

Thiridon's teacher read Bible stories to the children every day. She taught them how to pray. Because of her teacher, Thiridon has learned to love Jesus. She loves to attend the little Adventist church in her village, and now she even leads many activities in church.

Thiridon's love for God is contagious. She invites her friends to come to church programs, and many of them do. She invited her older brother, Saw, to church, and he came. He gave his heart to Jesus and recently was baptized.

Enthusiastic supporter

When the district pastor announced that the church would show some Christian videos to teach the people about God, Thiridon could hardly wait. The people in her village are very poor and do not own television sets. So when the pastor announced the Christian videos, Thiridon wanted everyone to come to the programs. She knew they would enjoy them. She began by inviting her family to attend; then she invited her school friends to come. She even went from door to door inviting the neighbors to come.

One boy whom Thiridon invited to church to see the videos was Maung Sa Tin (MONG-sah-tihn). He came to the church, and after learning for himself how much God loves him, he gave his life to Jesus. He is looking forward to being baptized soon and becoming a member of God's family. "I am glad that Thiridon invited me," he said. "I will invite others to come to church now too."

Best friends

Thiridon's best friend is Thanda Aye (THAHN-dah ai). Thiridon invited her to come to church on Sabbath too. Every Sabbath morning Thanda Aye comes to Thiridon's house, and the girls walk to church together. Thanda Aye's parents are not Adventists, but they allow Thanda Aye to attend the Adventist church because they have seen how well behaved Thiridon is. The two girls often talk about how they can help their parents learn to love God. They have promised each other that they will ask God to help them show their parents that an Adventist Christian is a happy, joyful person. They often pray together that their parents and friends will give their lives to God.

A shining star for God

Thiridon is a shining star for Jesus. She prays for her friends and invites them to church programs. She wants to be like Jesus. She is helpful at home and does her schoolwork willingly and well. And she prays for her family and friends. Most of all, she wants to be a happy, joyful shining star for God.

"Please pray for me," Thiridon asks. "And pray for my family and friends who do not know about Jesus yet. And please pray for my friend Thanda Aye and her family. We want our parents and brothers and sisters to be in heaven with us."

What can you do to be shining stars for Jesus, as Thiridon is? Let's start by praying that God will fill our hearts with His love and joy. Then everyone around us will know that Jesus is our best Friend.

Trans-European Division

A Love Letter From God

The boy thought God did not love him. Then he found a letter in a field.

Today's story is about a boy named Bart, from Sweden.

During family worship, Bart listened as his father told a story about a woman God saved when guerilla soldiers attacked the bus she and her son were riding in. Soldiers shot several people, but when a soldier came to the woman, he motioned for her to get off the bus and run into the bushes. She grabbed her son, and they hid in the bushes until the soldiers left. Suddenly a man appeared nearby.

"Follow me," the man said. He did not look like a soldier, so the mother followed him to the next town. The man pointed out the police station and told her to report the crime there. The mother looked in the direction the man pointed for a moment. When she turned to thank him, the man was gone.

God doesn't love me

When Bart's father finished the story, Bart said sadly, "God would never do that for me. He does not love me enough." Bart's father asked him why he thought God did not love him.

"I've prayed a lot that God will show me that He loves me," Bart said, "But God hasn't answered yet."

Bart's parents felt bad that Bart thought God did not love him. They prayed with him and asked that God would do something special for him. Bart's parents prayed when they were alone too.

The balloon

On Sunday morning Bart rode his bike into the country to help a farmer. Bart and the farmer rode in the farmer's truck to get some hay. On their way back to the farm, Bart saw a balloon lying in the field. "May I go get the balloon?" Bart asked the farmer.

"Not now," the farmer told him. "We have work to do."

At noon Bart rode his bike home for lunch. He stopped at the field to look for the balloon. He saw it bobbing lazily in the field. Bart jumped across the ditch and ran to where the balloon lay. He picked it up and found a card attached with a piece of string. On the card was a picture of a Bible story and a note that said, "The children of the Adventist Church want to tell you that God loves you." Bart stared at the card for a moment. It was written in Dutch, Bart's native language. *How did this get all the way to Sweden?* he wondered.

Bart grabbed the card and balloon and jumped back on his bike. He rode home and skidded to a stop. Still holding on to the card and balloon, he shouted to his mother, "Mom! I've got a letter from Holland!"

Mother hurried to the door to see what Bart was so excited about. "Look, Mom," he said, holding up the card. "A letter from Holland came on a balloon. I found it in a field."

The letter from God

Bart gave his mother the card, and she read the message as Bart explained where he had found it.

"Bart," Mother asked, "do you understand who this letter is from and what it is saying?" Bart looked at his mother for an explanation. "This letter is not from Holland. It's from God. He sent you an answer to your prayer. He is telling you how much He loves you!" Bart's eyes sparkled as he realized what his mother was saying.

"God sent *me* a letter?" He thought about how he had found the balloon lying still in the field. It had come more than a thousand miles to reach a young boy who needed a message of love straight from God. After that, Bart took more interest in family devotions, in reading the Bible, and in praying.

Later Bart's parents learned that some children in Holland had tied cards to balloons and let them go one Sabbath afternoon. There was little wind, and the children were sad that their cards would not make it very far. Bart's card apparently had traveled the farthest. When Bart found it, it had been lying in a field for at least an hour in clear view of children playing nearby. Yet, no one noticed it except Bart.

God *does* love us—each one of us. We can be God's letter of love to someone today.

Sad Little Duku

Sudan

A sad boy became a glad boy when God helped him find a way to attend Sabbath School again.

Duku *(DOO-coo)* grew up in a village in southern Sudan. He loved going to Sabbath School and tried never to be late. He loved to sing songs about Jesus and listen to Bible stories.

But one day something happened that made Duku very sad. His mother moved to another house, leaving Duku and his father alone. Duku missed his mother; he wished his parents were still living together. But his father told him that his mother was not happy living with them, and she did not want to come back.

Then one day Duku's father had to go on a trip. He took Duku to stay with his mother. Duku loved his father, but he had missed his mother and was glad to be able to visit her for a while.

Everything has changed

But soon Duku noticed that his mother had changed. She was not as happy as she had been when the family lived together. When Sabbath came, Duku got up and dressed in his good clothes, ready to walk to Sabbath School. But his mother did not get dressed. "Aren't you going to church today?" Duku asked, surprised. Duku's mother said she was too busy to take him to church.

"Mother, please go to church with me," Duku begged. But his mother refused and told him to go outside and play. "Why don't you want to go to church with me, Mama?" Duku asked.

Duku's mother became angry and told him, "Don't tell me what to do. Now go outside and leave me alone!"

Duku went outside and sat down in the shade of a little tree. He thought about the children who would be going to Sabbath School; he wished that he could be there too. But he did not know how to get to the church by himself.

The next Sabbath Duku again asked his mother to take him to Sabbath School, and again she refused, and again Duku sat under the tree with tears flowing down his cheeks.

Why are you crying?

Duku's neighbor, a young man named Isaac, noticed Duku. "Why are you crying?" Isaac asked.

Duku stood up and wiped his cheeks with his hand. "I want to go to church, but my mother won't take me," he said.

Just then Duku's mother stepped out of her little house. "Why don't you take Duku to church?" he asked her. But Duku's mother refused to talk about it.

Week after week Isaac watched Duku sit outside his *tukul* *(TOO-cool)*—his hut—crying on Saturday morning. Isaac could not stand to see Duku so sad. He marched to Duku's mother's tukul and asked her, "May I take Duku to church this morning?"

Duku's mother was a little surprised, but finally she agreed. "I'm too busy to be bothered to take him," she said.

Duku was overjoyed that Isaac would take him to Sabbath School. Week after week Isaac and Duku went to church together. Soon they were going to midweek services, Sabbath vespers, even choir practice together!

Now, Isaac was not an Adventist, but he enjoyed the church services as much as Duku did. Soon he joined the Bible-study class, and one day Isaac told Duku that he had decided to become a member of the church Duku loved so much.

A change of heart

Week after week Duku's mother watched Isaac take her son to the church that she had once attended. She listened as Duku told her the Bible story he had learned in Sabbath School and sang the songs he loved. Little by little Duku's mother began to wish for the happy days when the family worshiped God together.

Duku began to notice that Mother was changing. Instead of brewing beer to sell, she began baking bread and knitting table covers to sell. And one day when Duku asked his mother to go to church with him, she accepted.

Mother began attending church with Duku and Isaac every Sabbath. And several months later, when Duku's father returned home, Mother and Duku moved back home with him. On Sabbath morning Duku sat between his mother and father in church and smiled. At last they are a happy family worshiping God together, just as they should. And Isaac was glad that he had taken pity on a sad little boy and had taken him to church.

Is there someone in your home or your neighborhood that you can invite to church this week? You'll be glad you did.

West-Central Africa Division

Basile's Discovery

Benin

*"Papa, please come and listen to the music down the road!
It is so beautiful!"*

Basile *(bah-SEEL)* lives in the country of Benin in western Africa. His father, whom he calls Papa, believed in voodoo, a form of witchcraft that is common in western Africa. Papa kept voodoo gods in the house to protect the family from evil spirits that might want to harm them. Papa worshiped the gods of water, thunder, snakes, trees, and the devil, and many more. At Papa's work, the men often argued about which gods provided the best protection against the evil spirits.

Beautiful music

One day as Basile walked along the street, he heard singing and stopped to listen. It was beautiful! Basile turned and ran home, calling, "Papa, Papa! Come hear the beautiful music down the road!" Papa was busy, but he laid down his tools and followed his son into the street.

Papa and Basile could hear the music before they could see the choir. They stood a short distance away and listened until the singing stopped. Then they saw two men step into a large concrete tank filled with water. One man raised his hand and spoke some words. Then he pushed the other man under the water! But before Papa could react, the first man lifted the other man up from the water and hugged him! Basile and his father had never seen a ceremony quite like this before, and they thought it was strange voodoo. As they turned to leave, the choir sang another song.

A man stepped up to Papa and invited him to return the next Saturday. "We would be happy to have you," the man said.

Papa thanked the man and turned toward home. "Papa," Basile said, "may I come back again next week and hear the music again? It was so beautiful!"

"Yes, son, you may return," Papa answered. "Just don't let anyone put you in that water."

Learning about Jesus

Basile attended the worship service the following week. He enjoyed the happy music and loved the stories he heard about Jesus. Week after week he attended the meetings, returning home to tell his family what he had learned. He invited his family to join him, and his mother and sisters started going to church with Basile every Sabbath.

Then one day Basile came home from church with a serious look on his face. "Papa," he said, "the pastor said that voodoo fetishes have no power of their own. He said their power comes from the devil, and the devil is not as strong as Jesus, God's Son. If that is true, we should worship Jesus, not the fetishes."

Basile's oldest brother was not pleased that his family was turning away from the voodoo gods. He wanted to show his family that Christians don't know everything. He decided to shame the church's pastor by asking him questions that he could not answer. So on Sabbath, Basile's brother went to church with the family. After church his brother asked the pastor many questions, trying to show that the pastor was not so smart. But the pastor opened his Bible and read texts to answer each question. Basile's brother realized that he was the not-so-smart one. He started attending church to listen and to learn. In time Basile's brother, along with his mother and his sisters, accepted Jesus as their Lord and joined the Adventist Church.

Papa got rid of his gods and their fetishes, and he accepted Jesus as his Savior too. But he could not be baptized because he had two wives.

Trial and victory

Then one of Basile's aunts became sick. Her family paid the voodoo priests to get rid of the evil spirits that were making her sick, but she did not get better. Even the doctor at the clinic could not cure her. Finally she asked Papa to pray for her. Papa asked God to heal his sister. God answered this prayer, and Basile's aunt was healed.

Other members of the family realized that Basile's Papa's God was more powerful than the voodoo they practiced. Basile's aunt began attending church and was baptized with two of her children.

When Papa's second wife went home to her village, Papa could be baptized. Now the whole family is united in Jesus, all because young Basile believed in Jesus and shared God's love with his family.

Basile shared his faith with others. You can share your faith with your family and friends too.

Samuel's Singing Band

Ghana

Samuel and his friends wanted to share God's love with others, but doing so got them into big trouble.

Samuel lives in a city in northern Ghana. He loves God, and he loves to sing. He loves using music to help others know about Jesus. But one time Samuel's love for God and for Christian music got him into trouble.

Sharing their faith

Samuel and some of his friends liked to hold pretend church services in a shed that they built. They took turns pretending to be the pastor, the song leader, and the congregation. One day Samuel thought about how much better it would be if they actually told people about God instead of just pretending. The boys decided to practice their music and go from house to house singing Christian songs for people. "We thought it would make them happy, and if they asked us to tell them more about Jesus, we could give them a tract or a little book," Samuel explained.

The boys decided to try out their plan. They walked to a nearby neighborhood and sang some songs on the street. When they saw people sitting in the shade of a tree or on their porch, they sang for them. Then they walked into the courtyard of one home and started to sing. As they were singing, a boy walked toward them and started singing with them. He was singing the same song, but he sang bad words instead of the right words. Some of the words were ones Christians would never use! Samuel and his friends kept singing their song, hoping the newcomer would go away or stop singing bad words.

The angry teacher

A teacher lived in the house where the group was singing. He heard the Christian music, but he also heard the bad words. The bad words made the man angry, and he walked to the door and tossed a pitcher of cold water on the boys. "What are you kids doing here?" he shouted. "You sing Christian songs, but you mock God by using bad words! Go away!"

The boy who had sung the bad words ran away, but Samuel and his friends stayed. Samuel knew he and his friends had done nothing wrong. Samuel tried to explain to the man that they were not the ones who had sung the bad words. They did not want the teacher to think they were making fun of God when they were really trying to honor God!

The teacher stepped out of the house, but he refused to let Samuel explain what had happened. He called Samuel and his friends bad boys and ordered them to leave his yard.

Samuel felt terrible. He did not want the teacher to think that they were making fun of God. But the more the boys tried to explain, the angrier the teacher became. Finally he threatened to come to their school and tell the teacher to whip the boys!

In big trouble

Samuel and his friends started toward home. They knew that their teacher would listen to this man's accusations and punish them without giving the boys a chance to explain what had really happened.

Sure enough, on Monday the boys were called to the headmaster's office. There stood the teacher who had yelled at them. He had told the headmaster what he thought they had done, and the headmaster punished them all. Now not only the teacher thought they were bad, but the headmaster of their school thought the boys had done something bad too. Samuel knew that their parents would hear of the trouble and be ashamed if they thought the boys had really done this bad deed.

But Samuel and his friends were not ready to give up trying to clear their names, especially with this teacher. Samuel decided to tell his parents what had happened before the headmaster could tell them. Fortunately, Samuel's parents knew about the singing band, and he knew that they would believe him.

Truth at last

Mother listened to Samuel's explanation of what had happened. "Let's all go back to the teacher's house and talk to him," Mother said in that tone of voice that Samuel understood to mean he had little choice. So the six boys met at Samuel's house. They prayed that God would open the teacher's mind and heart so he would listen to the truth. Then Samuel's parents and the boys walked to the teacher's house.

At first the teacher did not want to talk to Samuel's parents or the boys, but finally his parents convinced the man to listen to Samuel. As politely as he could, Samuel told the teacher what had really happened that day. "Talk to any of us, and we will tell you the same thing," Samuel said bravely.

The teacher thought for a moment, then asked each boy what had happened. One boy knew the boy who had caused the trouble, and he told the teacher his name. The teacher found the boy and questioned him about what had happened. The boy hung his head and refused to answer the teacher. The teacher realized that he had punished the wrong boys.

The teacher threatened to have the other boy whipped—harder than Samuel and his friends had been. But Samuel said, "No, the Bible says do not repay evil with evil." So the teacher agreed not to punish the boy.

Surprise visit

The teacher did two things that surprised Samuel. First he went to Samuel's home to apologize. He said he wanted to be Samuel's friend. Then he went to the school and told the headmaster that the boys who had been punished were innocent.

When Samuel learned that the teacher had visited the headmaster, Samuel said, "Let's go to his house again and sing for him!" The boys went, and the teacher was impressed. After all, he had punished them for something they had not done.

The boys invited the teacher to church—and he went! He was impressed with the church and kept attending. Today he is a member of Samuel's church. Now when the boys go house to house singing, the teacher goes with them.

Important lessons

Samuel has learned some important lessons from what happened. "Singing can lead people to Jesus, just like preaching and praying can," Samuel said. "When you have trouble, sing; when you feel joy, sing. And if someone says you did something wrong, be careful how you respond. It could make the difference between the person becoming an enemy or a brother or sister in Christ!"

If you enjoyed this book, you'll want to read these mission stories too.

Curse-Proof!
Eric B. Hare

A little woman with a rope in her hand sprang from the veranda and ran screaming into the forest.

"Look, look, it's Mother!" screamed the two sisters. "She's going into the jungle to hang herself!"

They gave a withering look at their brother, Maung Thein, and shouted, "It's all your fault! It's all your fault! You've driven your mother mad, and if she commits suicide, we'll call you a murderer!"

The village people gathered and asked, "Why don't you undo it? Why don't you undo this baptism?"

You'll be inspired by Eric B. Hare's story of a young man's unshakeable faith.

ISBN 13: 978-0-8163-2208-4   ISBN 10: 0-8163-2208-2
Paperback, 96 pages.

Mission Miracles
Eileen E. Lantry with David and Becky Gates

"Precious Lord, surely You haven't brought us this far to let everything fail!"

David Gates lay awake at night agonizing about the $1.4 million due in a short time. Had they been wrong to write the check knowing that there was no money yet to cover it?

His wife, Becky, also wrestled over the huge debt, which was for the purchase of a television network. . . . "Dear Jesus, please tell us, what shall we do?"

Instantly, God responded to her plea, giving her the promise in Deuteronomy 33:27. "The eternal God is your refuge, and underneath are the everlasting arms."

ISBN 13: 978-0-8163-2186-5   ISBN 10: 0-8163-2186-8
Paperback, 208 pages

Three ways to order:
1. Local Adventist Book Center®
2. Call 1-800-765-6955
3. Shop AdventistBookCenter.com